LIFE SKILLS FOR TEENS TOOLKIT

PROVEN STRATEGIES TO BUDGET WISELY, SAVE WITHOUT STRESS, BUILD HEALTHY RELATIONSHIPS, AND PLAN A SUCCESSFUL CAREER WITH CONFIDENCE AND LASTING PERSONAL GROWTH

ELLA MURPHY

CONTENTS

Introduction   5

1. MASTERING FINANCES   13
Budgeting Made Simple   14
Smart Saving and Investing   19
Taxes Decoded   23
Loans Decoded   26
Credit Cards and Building Credit   29
Renting Know-How   33
Hands-On Element: Create Your Personal
Budget Plan   38

2. CAREER PATH FINDING   41
Choosing Your Path   42
Tackling Career Uncertainty   45
Resume Building   49
Hands-On Element: Develop Your Personal Career
Exploration Plan   54

3. FOSTERING RELATIONSHIPS   57
Understanding Effective Communication   58
Practical Communication Strategies   67
Building Stronger Connections Through
Communication   71
Hands-On Element: Enhance Your Communication
Skills   75

4. PERSONAL GROWTH AND DEVELOPMENT   77
Cultivating Self-Worth and Confidence   78
Embracing Health and Wellness   88
Organizational Mastery   92
Hands-On Element: Cultivate Your Personal
Growth Plan   95

5. ESSENTIAL DAILY LIVING SKILLS   99
Navigating Groceries and Cooking   100
Vehicle Know-How   104

Being Emergency Ready — 108
Hands-On Element: Developing Your Daily Living Skills — 114

6. TRAVEL WISDOM — 117
Travel Planning and Budgeting — 118
Passport and Global Exploration — 120
Insurance and Safety Essentials — 123
Hands-On Element: Crafting Your Personal Travel Plan — 127

7. DIGITAL LITERACY AND SAFETY — 131
Navigating the Digital World — 132
Online Safety and Privacy — 136
Leveraging Digital Tools for Success — 141
Hands-On Element: Enhancing Your Digital Competence — 144

8. GOING GREEN: YOUR GUIDE TO ECO-FRIENDLY LIVING — 147
Understanding Environmental Impact — 148
Practicing Sustainable Living — 153
Advocacy and Community Involvement — 156
Hands-On Element: Embracing Sustainable Practices in Daily Life — 164

Conclusion — 169
References — 175

Once we were young, now we are adults.

LAILAH GIFTY AKITA

We're all guilty of excitedly anticipating the grand finale of high school where that graduation cap goes all airborne, and *bam!* You're an adult!

Oh, the freedom, and I mean, unlimited space to be yourself? So much to look forward to, right? Of course, there is! But, here's the reality check that they forget to mention about being a grown-up: There are bills, endless to-do lists, and a whole laundry list of other responsibilities that never made it onto the syllabus.

You see, the thing is, schools and teachers are there to educate you, *not raise you.* It's all about algebra and Shakespeare, and not so much about turning you into an independent, responsible, fully functioning adult. That's the parents "job." However, associate research scientist with the University of Michigan and co-director of the C.S. Mott Children's Hospital National Poll on Children's

Health, Sarah Clark, conducted a poll and found that parents aren't exactly acing it when it comes to prepping their teens for the big world out there. Now, don't get me wrong, parents are awesome—they want nothing but the best for their kids. In fact, when Clark asked them in the poll, a whopping 87% of parents thought they were doing enough to prepare their children for the great escape from the nest (Thompson, 2019). Ironically, here's where things get interesting: Those same parents also doubted their teens' abilities when it came to handling the basics of adulting. It's like saying, "Yes, you've got this, but not quite." Talk about mixed signals!

Yup, according to the poll, parents seem to struggle with believing in their children's life skills because they're not too sure about their own strategies for nurturing those crucial skills (Thompson, 2019). So, despite all the struggles, what are these skills?

Well, well, well, do you understand the fundamentals of taxes? You know, those sneaky little things lurking around the corner, ready to pounce on your paycheck? It's a total ambush of tax forms and regulations! And just when you think you've got it all figured out, *bam*! Another curveball comes flying your way. It's the mysterious art of groceries!

Gone are the days of leisurely strolling down the aisles, debating between the swashbuckling boxes of Lucky Charms and the adventures of Captain Crunch. Nope, now it's all about deciphering the cryptic labels and unraveling the differences between whole wheat and multigrain while juggling your nutritional needs and sticking to a budget. Sounds like a real "cereal killer," right? And, what the heck is quinoa anyway? Welcome to the thrilling world of adulting!

And, what's the parents' take on this? According to Clark's eye-opening poll on their thoughts about their teens' skills, the following played out (Thompson, 2019):

- 8% of parents were confident their teen could successfully nail an appointment with a doctor on their own.
- 25% of parents thought their teen could accurately measure the correct dose of over-the-counter medication without chugging a bottle of cough syrup like it's soda pop.
- 41% of parents banked on their teens opting for healthier food.
- 46% of parents believe their teens will stash some cash for the future.
- 50% of parents believed their teens could handle a minor injury with first aid.
- 65% of parents thought their teens would get enough sleep to maintain their health, avoiding the siren call of Netflix binges and late-night TikTok scrolling.

Looks like there's a lot on the parental worry radar. It gets even more interesting with this poll. When the parents were asked why their kids weren't ready for independence, guess what they said (Thompson, 2019)?

- Three in five "momagers and dadagers" said the problem lies with their teen not being ready for independence.
- 14% of parents think their teen doesn't know enough to handle their own business.
- 25% of parents felt that they were the barrier standing between their teen and independence.
- 19% of parents admitted that things are just a whole lot easier if they take care of business themselves instead of leaving it up to their teen.

Spotting an odd cycle here? Clark brings up an interesting point—it's like this never-ending loop where teens aren't given the chance to learn independence because they're not considered knowledgeable enough to handle it. It's that all-familiar mindset of "it's easier if I just do it myself."

Despite the adversity, where does this leave everyone? It might be fine and well right now, life's a breeze, but what's really happening is that independence is slowly slipping away. It's time to step up and own your independence. It's a true investment when you can manage yourself, and that pays off big time. Life is easier if you can have everything done for you. I mean, who wants to engage in challenges and debates every day, right? But, in the real world, you have to roll up your sleeves, do things for yourself, and make things happen. Otherwise, life will pass you by instead of working in your favor.

It is imperative now, parent or teen, we're all in this together. No need for the blame game here. As "the rents," it's on us to carve out the time and effort to invest in our teens. And for you, as teenagers, being open and eager to learn and invest in yourself is equally as important. It's about feeling confident in your abilities and not only owning but earning your independence.

Independence is not solely hinged on having the ability to earn a "fat" paycheck and living in the big wide world on your own. It's more holistic. It's about living responsibly, effectively, and successfully. You are standing on the brink of independence, equipped with dreams and aspirations. However, there is a critical component that often gets overlooked amidst the hustle of academics and extracurriculars: life-long, life skills.

It's life! It gets complex and you, as a teenager, need a wide range of abilities to handle what comes your way with competence and confidence. Why? Because you deserve to live your best life possible! You must learn to be financially literate, communicate properly, manage your time sufficiently, and be self-aware enough to approach problem-solving.

We find ourselves in a time where the world is hyper-connected! It's a double-edged sword where life has become more relentless, yet we are grateful for the wealth of information and friends at our fingertips. It's almost as if we're living in two realities at once. Honestly, we might be! We are so happy about the convenience and the variety. However, at the same time, it has also turned into a "drive-through" culture of instant gratification, making these life skills all the more important.

We're living in a time where student loan debt is skyrocketing and the economy is volatile, highlighting the critical importance of managing finances wisely, budgeting effectively, and making informed money decisions. Yet, many teens graduate without grasping the basics, leaving them vulnerable to financial pitfalls. Let's take effective communication, which is so important in this interconnected "double reality" of ours. Think networking for career opportunities, building meaningful relationships, or advocating for yourself. Strong communication skills are essential for success in virtually every aspect of modern-day life. You need more than memorization and the ability to pass standardized testing.

Sure, academic knowledge has its place, but it's equally as important, as a teenager, to take it upon yourself to equip yourself with the practical tools and abilities you need to thrive in today's complex world. And, might I add that the landscape of teenage life has changed just as swiftly as the world around us. Just twenty years ago, a typical teen might have been riding a bike, able to spot poison ivy, and likely had a part-time job to earn pocket money for that shiny new bike they wanted. Fast forward to today, and teens are coding and expert selfie editors, with pocket money and the latest cell phone; it's almost a given. It's as if the ability to do things for oneself has become drowned out by the allure of filters and the flood of fake news on social platforms.

You have to keep up with the times; however, a lot of the simple, very vital aspects have fallen to the wayside, such as those all-important life skills. Recent studies have shown a noticeable decline in traditional "adult" activities among teenagers today, indicating that they are becoming less prepared for adulthood with each passing generation (Twenge, 2017). But, what's driving all of this? I bet you more than half of people will say it's the onslaught of modern technology and smartphones that have changed the way we interact and communicate. Sure, that's a valid point, however, blaming the rise of technology alone is not going to make any problems magically disappear. What's going to happen if we were to eliminate all the smartphones from all teenagers? Unplugging may help to some extent, but how are they going to pick up skills like problem-solving and leadership that are all key aspects of a successful life?

There's more to this equation than just removing things and shifting blame. It's not a one-sided endeavor, rather it's a collective effort where we all need to stand together. Yes, adults today are merely borrowing the world from our children and we must make sure we instill the proper skills in them, enabling them to instill the same valuable skills in future generations. And, you, as a teenager, need to actively adopt these skills and seek to learn them so you can leave a better future for your children and the generations to come. It's a collective responsibility that each of us has to personally take on to be the best versions of ourselves, enabling us to live fulfilled lives. It's not just a responsibility, it's a moral footprint and a legacy that we all leave behind, one that will endure long beyond our years.

At the end of the day, we're all in this together; educators, parents, and teenagers.

And, here it is, right in your very hands: a structured approach, filled with interactive elements and practical advice to navigate vital life skills, all aimed at living a responsible, fulfilled life and leaving that important moral legacy. We are going to take a look at mastering the fine art of finances, discovering the perfect career fit, and uncovering some travel wisdom. And, let's not overlook the personals; we'll also explore what healthy relationships entail, delve into personal growth and development, and cover those "can't-live-without" daily life skills. Oh, and then we'll pivot to going not only "green" but also "digital" exploring eco-friendly living and becoming savvy "digizens," or digital citizens.

We all hear about these aspects and I, undoubtedly, know that you've stumbled across them too. But this time, it's different. I'm presenting it all in a functional, easily understandable manner, eliminating the enigma aspect. Whether you're a parent or a teenager, you'll find it easy to incorporate these principles into your life.

You are the next generation, and you need to empower yourself! Having a firm grasp on foundational skills is the building blocks that help construct a successful adulthood. And, this one's for the parents: You're not raising a child, you're raising an adult!

But, before we forge ahead, I want to clear the air and mention that I am talking directly to you, as a teen, ready to embark on this journey known as life. Stay on course, take your time, the content is dense...but the rewards are endless.

CHAPTER ONE

MASTERING FINANCES

Have you ever wondered why financial stress seems like it's a constant companion for many folks out there? Simply put, it's often because money ends up calling the shots instead of people taking clever shots with their money!

Yup, so many folks hand over the keys to their financial kingdom, allowing cash to rule the roost because, well, they're pretty clueless when it comes to financial management. And, you know what? There's absolutely no need to live from paycheck to paycheck. You can account for every penny with your long-term goals in mind!

So, are you ready to live life on your own financial terms, one dollar at a time instead of the other way around? Of course, you are!

BUDGETING MADE SIMPLE

Budgeting is a strategic plan detailing how you intend to allocate your money. And, the sooner you start properly managing your finances, the better. Otherwise, you might just end up eating ramen noodles for the rest of your life.

Being able to budget properly is not just about tracking your cash, it's about gaining financial freedom! When you know where every precious penny flows, it contributes to your independence along the way. Yes, life is all about needs and wants, but when it comes to money, it's all about needs, wants, and savings.

Mastering the art of budgeting and making your dollars stretch might require some time and patience but, as challenging as curbing your spending impulses may be, failing to grasp the basics of budgeting at an earlier age can create a snowball of woes later in adulthood. This could include mismanaged funds, mounting debt, minimal to nonexistent savings, and heaps of stress.

Forget about adopting budgeting skills when you move out. You need them now! It's important to understand the four key components—income, expenses, savings and investments, and debt— and how to integrate them into your financial plan.

And, as with everything, to attain success, you need a plan that works.

Creating a Personalized Budget

There are a couple of things you have to tick off when it comes to understanding how to conjure up a solid financial plan. So, let's roll out the red carpet and kick off with a star-studded lineup of essential elements to create your perfect fit.

- **Income:** First things first, calculate the average income you rake in every month. This will include all the money that comes rolling into your bank account, from your allowance to those sweet, sweet paychecks. Exclude any occasional bonuses, such as birthday money or little cash surprises from the grandparents.
- **Expenses:** Calculate all your expenses for a month to know where the moolah flows. Use apps, spreadsheets, or even receipts to track what you're splurging on each month.
- **Patterns:** After pinning down your income and expenses, it's time to spot patterns. Look at your expenses and split them into two camps: necessities (like phone bills and transport) and nice-to-haves (like Netflix subscriptions and hanging out with friends). This will give you a picture of where you can tighten the purse strings and cut down on costs.
- **Budget:** This is the big reveal! Deduct your necessities total from your income. The rest of the amount that's left is what you have to allocate to savings and non-essentials.
- **Saving:** A good rule of thumb is to squirrel away at least 20% of what's left for your savings. That way, you're set up for future goals and ready to tackle any unexpected expenses that might come your way. Set up savings buckets in your apps or set up automatic transfers.
- **Methods:** There are heaps of savings strategies out there:

  - 50/30/20 rule
  - Zero-based budgeting
  - Reverse budgeting
  - Envelope budgeting
  - Do a bit of research and explore various options to find that perfect fit.

- **Implement:** Get that budget locked in and adjust your spending habits accordingly. Stick to the plan!
- **Review:** Your budget's a living, breathing thing. It will require regular reviews and adjustments as your income and necessities fluctuate. Ensure that you make necessary, realistic adjustments to keep it consistently aligned with your financial goals, maintaining effectiveness.

Here's a solid example of a monthly budget that will help track your estimated and actual income and expenses for a month:

Category	Monthly Budget	Actual Amount	Difference
INCOME			
Wages and income	$220	$230	+$10
Interest income	$8	$6	(-$2)
INCOME SUBTOTAL	$228	$236	+$8
EXPENSES			
Savings: money for savings	$15	$15	$0
Bills			
Taxes: from your paycheck	$35	$37	(-$2)
Rent	$10	$10	$0
Utilities: water, electricity, etc.	$35	$35	$0
Groceries and snacks	$20	$18	+$2
Car			
Car Payment	$10	$10	$0
Car Insurance	$15	$15	$0
Gasoline	$25	$30	(-$5)
Shopping			
Clothes	$45	$40	+$5
Other Shopping	$12	$5	+$7
Fun			
Entertainment: restaurants, movies, video games, etc.	$25	$30	(-$5)
Other Expenses			
Tennis club	$12	$12	$0
EXPENSES SUBTOTAL	$259	$254	+$5
NET INCOME			
Income Minus Expenses	$31	$37	+$6

Adapting Budgeting Strategies

Life's filled with surprises and very few guarantees, including income stability, so having adaptable budgeting strategies in place is an absolute must-have!

- First, cover all the necessities such as rent, food, and transportation.
- Create a realistic budget based on your typical monthly average income.
- If your pay fluctuates, budget based on your lowest earnings just to play it safe.
- Pay yourself a monthly allowance for expenses from your income account to avoid the overspending trap.
- Build an emergency fund, even if it's just a little bit each month. Keep it consistent, you're investing in your future!
- Around the holidays or back-to-school season, expenses tend to skyrocket. Be sure to save up a bit extra during the good months.
- Use tax refunds and birthday money to bulk up your savings when you can.
- Saving every single month with a fluctuating income can be rather challenging. However, time and compound interest boost those small, regular amounts.
- Opt for a Tax-Free Savings Account (TFSA), which is flexible enough to invest money from irregular income.
- Automate payments, including savings, for simplicity.
- Keep track of your income changes.
- Check out the 50/30/20 budget rule:

  - 50% for the must-haves
  - 30% for the fun stuff
  - 20% for savings and debt

The key lies in balancing your needs and savings. Sure, it may require discipline and patience, but you're essentially buying your future financial freedom.

SMART SAVING AND INVESTING

When it comes to growing your money, you have more options than a squirrel in a peanut factory!

You can stash your cash in a basic savings account or go full out and try your hand at stocks. However, as a beginner, mutual funds and ETFs let you tap into multiple stocks without crazy risks. Then, there are bonds, which are loans paying *you* interest based on rates. For the more patient disciplined folks, compounding interest is great as a long-term option. At the end of the day, it's all about educating yourself, starting small, and staying sensible.

But, let's take a closer look.

Saving and Investing Basics

Here are a couple of practical savings tips:

- The first secret to saving is that it's best to pay off any debt before you play the investment game. Additionally, ensure that you have enough savings to cover your living expenses for at least six months in case of unexpected emergencies.

Now, for some investment basics:

- Avoid inflating your lifestyle with your income, and resist splurging on fancy things. Instead, save and invest your extra cash.

- It's never too early to start investing your money, even if it's just a small amount that will enable your money to grow over time.
- Have clear goals for your money to help you pin down the best investment strategy. Are you saving for retirement, college, or something else?
- Understand the risks and how much you're willing to take before parting with your money.
- Never put all your eggs in one basket. Spread your investments across different investments to reduce risks.
- Keep an eye out for the fees you're paying to avoid them eating into returns.

Types of Investments

What are your options when it comes to investing?

- **Bonds:** Think of bonds as IOUs, where you lend money to a company or government, who, in turn, pays you back with interest on the original loan amount.
- **Stocks:** When you buy stocks, you're buying into a tiny piece of a company. It can be rather risky, but stocks offer the potential for high returns.
- **Real estate:** This is all about buying properties or shares in real estate companies. While it carries risk, as most investments do, it offers the potential for lucrative returns.
- **Automated investing:** This is more of a hands-free approach, where your investments are managed by computer algorithms. You let it know what your goals and risk tolerance are, and it manages your investments automatically.

6 Accounts to Grow Your Money

When it comes to stashing your cash, look for a savings account that offers the best interest rates in simple terms. This means you'll have to keep a wide eye on basics such as fees, balance requirements, and interest rates.

Let's look at some options:

- **Traditional savings accounts:** You can get yourself one of these accounts from banks and credit unions, offering easy access, though interest rates are pretty low.
- **High-yield savings accounts:** You have to stick to withdrawal limits and be comfortable navigating online banking, but you can expect some higher interest rates compared to a traditional savings account.
- **Certificates of deposit (CDs):** If you're willing to lock in your money without needing immediate access, CDs provide excellent fixed interest rates for set periods.
- **Money market accounts (MMAs):** These are great if you're looking for higher interest rates without locking in your funds.
- **Cash management accounts:** Managed online, these accounts earn competitive interest rates and allow both savings and investments in one account, making them ideal for maximizing cash while keeping it mixed with investments.
- **Specialty savings accounts:** This is a purpose-driven account where you get to save toward specific goals, such as tuition, with potentially FDIC-insured benefits.

Strategic Saving

- **Start small and think big by setting smaller, achievable goals.** For instance, aim for $200, then $500, and then $1000, increasing your targets over time. Aiming to save 20% of a $50,000 salary could build a substantial emergency fund within a few years. Not only will this keep you motivated, but also think of all the possibilities that come with having a safety net!
- **Create a solid mental barrier between your everyday spending and savings by popping your savings funds into a separate account.** This will help curb those impulse buys, ensuring you always have cash stashed away for a rainy day.
- **Whenever you receive extra cash injections, such as birthday money or tax refunds, don't blow it all on frivolous treats.** Pop that moolah straight into your emergency savings.
- **There's a big difference between wanting something and truly needing something.** Learn the fine art of distinguishing before splurging. Do you really need that trendy gadget, or is it just a case of FOMO (Fear Of Missing Out)? This will help you cut back on those unnecessary expenses that add up.
- **Regularly check in and review your budget to be sure it always aligns with your income and savings goals.** Prevention is always better than a financial emergency!
- **Only use your emergency funds for an emergency!** You don't want to deplete your savings and leave yourself vulnerable to the unforeseen. Let me reiterate: Make your money work for you, not the other way around.
- **Plan for the future and keep long-term financial goals in mind such as college or retirement.** Look into options

such as employer-sponsored plans like the 401(k), which offers convenient ways to save with potential employer matches and tax advantages.

- **For college, you can make use of a 529 plan, which offers tax benefits and flexible contribution limits.** These plans can help you cover your tuition, housing, and a variety of other educational expenses.
- **Then, there is the Roth IRA savings account, which you can use for retirement, tuition, or other goals.** This nifty tool lets you access your contributions penalty-free when needed.

TAXES DECODED

Let's talk about the big "T," as in taxes! It's all the deductions you see on your paycheck and the two main players are federal and state income taxes.

Think of federal taxes as the big daddy who funds things on a national level, such as social security and the military. The catch with federal income tax is that the more you make, the more they take. For instance, if you're single and make less than $11,000, you pay 10% of that to Uncle Sam. But, if you rake in over $500k, get ready to part with over 37%!

Then, there are state income taxes, which differ from state to state in the U.S. Some have a standard flat rate, meaning everyone pays the same percentage, while others operate like federal taxes, where the more you make, the more they take.

Having a solid grasp on the basics of federal and state income taxes is a good start for adulting! So, let's look at some basics of the US Tax System, including W3 and W2 forms:

W3 Form

- This form is a summary of all the information that employers use to spill the beans on employees' annual wages and tax information to the Social Security Administration (SSA).
- It sums up the total wages paid to all the employees during the year, including Social Security tax, federal income tax, and Medicare tax amounts withheld.
- Your employers will typically submit the W3 form along with copies of your W2 forms.

W2 Form

- This is also referred to as the Wage and Tax Statement, which is provided by your employer, reporting your annual wages and tax withholdings.
- It sums up your total wages earned, federal income tax withheld, Social Security and Medicare taxes withheld, as well as other deductions such as retirement plan contributions.
- The information on your W2 form is used to prep your individual tax returns and report your income to the Internal Revenue Service (IRS).

Filing Personal Taxes

Ah, IRS tax forms! Come on, it can be as overwhelming as choosing an ice cream flavor! Lucky for you, educating yourself about a couple of the big players will get you well on your way. After all, you wouldn't want to sign something without knowing what it is, right?

Here's a couple you'll want to know about:

Forms

- You may not need to file taxes yet, but it's important to understand the basics. Most people use the 1040 or 1040-SR form to report their income, deductions, and credits to the government.

Filing Your Federal Tax Return

- **Gather all necessary documents:** This will include all your forms and receipts, such as W2s from every employer, additional income statements (like 1099 and 1099-INT forms), and receipts for things you can subtract from your taxes.
- **Pick your filing status:** Are you single, married, or living with your parents? Based on your living situation, choose the appropriate filing status, which essentially affects how you'll file your taxes. Your choice impacts the amount of taxes you owe and the deductions you can claim. Courtesy of Uncle Sam!
- **How are you filing?** You can either opt for filing your taxes electronically by making use of tax preparation software recommended by the IRS. Alternatively, you can opt for filing via mail. But, remember "snail mail" may delay the process.
- **Standard deduction vs. itemizing:** Decide whether you are going to opt for the standard deduction, which is a fixed amount, or itemize your deductions, which means listing all your deductible expenses separately.
- **Payment:** Familiarize yourself with payment options,

including online payments, check or money orders, or exploring payment plan options if necessary.

- **Submission:** Keep your eyes on the filing deadline and be sure to submit your return in due time to avoid any penalties.
- **Track your refund:** You can check the status of your tax refund online after filing.
- **Seek assistance:** Visit the IRS website for answers or contact them by phone or in person at a Taxpayer Assistance Center office. You can also request help from your parents, trusted adults, or tax specialists.

If you're considering starting a business or becoming an entrepreneur, there are different tax opportunities and considerations to keep in mind. Business owners may be able to deduct certain expenses and take advantage of special tax breaks. But, business taxes can be complex, so it's wise to consult an accountant to help you navigate your specific tax situation. As you begin earning money and making financial decisions, stay informed and don't hesitate to seek advice when needed. Understanding the fundamentals of taxes and financial planning can help you make more informed decisions.

LOANS DECODED

Ah, the ever-popular student loan! But, tread with caution because none of the companies that put forth student loans do so for free; there's always the inevitable catch called "interest" involved. However, when it comes to money, the reality is, nothing comes for free.

Let's say you borrow $24,000 at a low interest rate of 2.5%, you will end up paying back $28,782 in total. Rather doable, right? But, if you're stuck with a higher interest rate, such as 10%, it could skyrocket your amount to over $48,000! That's a big leap. So, keep your eyes on that interest rate. There's always a price tag attached to *absolutely* everything in life.

Next up, you will have to consider time: The longer you take to pay off your loan, the more you will end up paying. Longer payment terms mean higher interest rates over time. And, last but not least, the more you borrow, the more you will be paying back. So, keep those eyes peeled on the interest rates, time, and loan amounts before signing away and taking out loans.

All's not doom and gloom because low-cost government loans are available for college. Yup, you heard it right. But, you need to know how to fill in the blanks regarding the FAFSA form to qualify and find your pot of gold at the end of this rainbow. It's a good shot to take when it comes to saving you and your family a bit of "greens."

Federal government loans are more flexible and affordable compared to others, but there are limits. For instance:

- **Your freshman year:** $5,500
- **Your sophomore year:** $6,500
- **Your junior year:** $7,500
- **Your senior year:** $7,500

Don't go getting all trigger-happy now because these limits work yearly, which means you can't borrow all the cash and hoard it. Nope, any extra funds won't roll over to the next year.

- **Pay back what you don't use ahead of time. Your money should work for you, remember?** Let's talk a bit of strategy: If it takes you five years to inch closer to your Bachelor's Degree, the amount you can borrow from the government that fifth year decreases. Unfortunately, you might have to rely more on higher-interest lenders for that extra year to cover tuition and other college costs, costing you more in the long run. Think about it!

- **Always weigh up your options.** Steer clear of high interest rates, read the fine print! Remember, these institutions are here to help, but it's never without a price tag attached.

SMART

Let's get SMART about the things we do in life, whether you're dealing with your cash flow or your personal stuff.

SMART goals offer cool strategies that you can employ in various aspects, such as finances, school, or career. They're super effective, providing a clear and structured framework. By making goals specific, measurable, achievable, relevant, and time-bound, you are keeping yourself motivated and accountable. Your goals will be structured with a well-defined and realistic approach.

Give it a shot!

- **Specific:** This is all about the "W" questions: who, what, when, where, which, and why. Be specific, and answer all your "W's" when it comes to setting your goals.
- **Measurable:** Your goals have to be quantifiable, enabling you to track your progress. Set realistic and measurable targets like saving $100 monthly, walking for 10 minutes each day, or taking a 10-minute tech detox. Baby steps! You can always build up from a realistic starting point.

- **Achievable:** Speaking of baby steps, keep your goals realistic! What tools, skills, and resources do you have at your disposal right now to get to the next level? You eat an elephant piece by piece, and the same goes for your goals, keep it manageable and realistic.
- **Relevant:** Keep it relevant in your life. Save for what will contribute in the longer run and align with your values. What values? Well, both monetary and principled, but we'll dive deeper into principles with further reading.
- **Time-bound:** You can take forever to hatch your egg, but that's not the aim of the game here, right? Set a deadline for your goals and stick to it to keep yourself driven and motivated. It's all about progress; celebrate even your smallest wins because they all contribute to your success in the end.

You always have one moment, and it's only in the present. Seize it!

CREDIT CARDS AND BUILDING CREDIT

What's a golden ticket? Well, apparently, a credit card! You know, that plastic thing that allows you to buy stuff without cash upfront? Sure, it sounds like a slice of heaven, but tread carefully, my young ones, for this plastic rectangle can submerge you into a whole lot of trouble if not used responsibly.

You see, a credit card works exactly like a debit card. The difference is though, that with a debit card when you buy something, you immediately pay for it and the money is deducted from your account. Credit. *Oi!* You can spend and pay later!

Yes, it's convenient and fun, plus you can use them for emergencies. They even come with cool rewards like cashback, discounts, and free flights! Add on to this, if you use them wisely, they can even boost your credit score. In all honesty, it's a double-edged sword that's totally dependent on your responsibility.

And, what makes it more enticing is the fact that there are so many to choose from:

- Regular credit cards have a spending limit and, at most, added rewards.
- Secured ones require a deposit for people without any bad credit.
- Reward cards with great spending perks.
- Balance transfer cards help move debt from one card to another with lower interest rates.

With so many options, how does one choose? Firstly, you want the fairest of the bunch, however, money and debt may truly become an ugly twin if you don't understand the simple math. Life's in the details they say.

Look at credit card interest rates, fees, customer service, and, of course, rewards. The procedure is pretty simple, and trust me, there will be plenty of people who'll help you part with your money.

Let's look into the process of applying for a credit card:

1. Explore all your different credit card options and choose the one that ticks most of your boxes.
2. Get all necessary documentation, such as proof of income, proof of residence, and identification.
3. You can pop online and visit the credit card company's website or visit a local branch to complete the application.
4. Fill out the form with your financial and personal information, submit it, and await the approval response.

Using Your Credit Card Responsibly

Using your credit card responsibly is very important because it will help you rack up a good credit score. But, what exactly does a credit score entail?

A credit score, typically ranging from 300 to 850, reflects your creditworthiness. This is also referred to as your FICO score; a type of credit score developed by the Fair Isaac Corporation (FICO). There are a lot of factors that come into play when determining your credit score, such as credit utilization, payment history, length of credit history, types of credit accounts, and new credit inquiries. Needless to say, a higher score means you're a lower credit risk, making it easier for you to qualify for loans, credit cards, and better interest rates. On the flip side, a poor credit score could make it tough to get the loans you need, such as for a car, tuition, or even rent a place to live.

Building a credit history takes time, so it's important to start working on establishing a good credit score as early as possible. Without it, the real world is a bit more challenging. Luckily, there are ways to begin:

- Ask a trusted family member to add you as an authorized user on a joint credit card.
- Look into secured credit cards where you put down a deposit upfront in exchange for card usage.

Remember, when you have your hands on your first credit card, you're in control of your rating. Stick to healthy money habits that will ensure you always have access to credit at the best rates possible! Here are a few tips:

- Pay on time! Set up automatic payments for recurring debts to avoid late payments that will reflect negatively on your credit record. These negative "blemishes" can stain your credit record for up to seven years!
- Pay more than the minimum balance to reduce interest charges and improve your credit score.
- Your credit utilization ratio (CUR) indicates how much of your available credit you use. Keep your CUR below 30% by using only a portion of your available credit.
- The type of credit you have also affects your score. So, diversify your credit portfolio with different types of credit accounts, such as installment loans, mortgages, and credit cards.
- Maintain a consistent track record of timely debt repayment. The longer track record you have of paying debts on time, the more likely you are to be deemed more creditworthy. Thus, hang onto that old credit card for the record.

Being Smart With Your Card

Let's look into a couple of additional tips that will help you be smart with your card:

- Stick to your budget like glue and steer clear from impulsive buys. Just because you have money at your disposal doesn't mean it's a shopping spree invitation. Think necessities, not luxuries.
- Never take cash advances unless it's for a "code red" emergency.
- Pay your bills in full to avoid any additional interest charges.
- And don't forget your credit card dictionary:

- ○ **Grace period:** The time allowance for paying off bills without extra charges.
- ○ **Credit limit:** The maximum amount you can borrow.
- ○ **APR:** This is the interest rate you pay per year on any money you owe.
- ○ **Balance transfer:** Moving debt from one card to another.
- ○ **Minimum Payment:** The smallest payable amount each month.

RENTING KNOW-HOW

It's exciting times when moving into your first abode. However, it also comes with a couple of head-scratchers. But, with a good plan, you can truly turn it into a smooth move!

Let's break it down:

Three Months Prior

- Figure out your monthly budget, which will include your rent and utility bills. Don't forget to include that initial security deposit.
- Hop online and look at listings to gauge prices, as moving can get expensive!
- If you need someone to co-sign your lease, make sure they're on board.

Two Months Prior

- Collect your pay stubs as proof of income.
- Round up a couple of potential living spots and chat with landlords about deposit deets. Ask the following questions to lock in your perfect option:

○ What are the terms of the lease? Make sure you know when the lease starts and ends, the monthly rent, and the late rent policy.

○ What are the move-in costs? Find out about the terms of your security deposit and any other additional fees, such as elevator or moving costs.

○ Does the rent include utilities, or are they paid separately?

○ Is there a pet policy?

○ What's the guest policy?

○ Do you need renters insurance? It's a good idea to have coverage for your belongings, even if it's not required.

○ How should rent be paid?

○ What are the maintenance and repair policies? Ask about response times for repairs, especially emergencies, and clarify responsibilities for maintenance.

○ How secure is the property and the neighborhood?

○ How often and by how much does the rent increase?

○ What is the parking policy?

○ What are the penalties for breaking the lease? Understand how to notify the landlord if you want to move out and the consequences for early termination of the contract.

- Consider off-peak moving times, there may be some good deals on rent.

One Month Prior

- Sign your lease and establish your move-in date.
- Plan your move logistics. Perhaps you would need a truck, or simply a couple of good friends.
- Start packing up your stuff and don't forget to label those boxes!

One to Three Weeks Prior

- If required, measure up your new spot to be sure your furniture will be a good fit.
- Update your mail forwarding and get your utilities in order, dotting all the I's and crossing the T's.

One Week Prior

- If you have a pet, be sure everything in your new place is set and ready to accommodate your furry friend.
- Pack up all your last-minute essentials and loose ends.

Moving Day

- Be calm, as moving can be tiring and tough.
- Thank everyone involved for lending a hand with pizza or a tip for the movers.
- Get the essentials in place first and the rest as you settle in.

Agreements and Documents

One of the most important documents you'll sign when moving into your own place is a lease. This is a legal agreement between you and the landlord that outlines all the terms and conditions for renting the property.

Leases can be verbal or in writing. However, having any agreement in writing, especially when parting with your money, is highly recommended. These agreements can differ from owner to owner, but there are a couple of things that come pretty standard with these contracts:

- Names and contact information of all parties involved.
- The agreed upon lease period.
- The monthly rental costs, including the date and form of payment.
- Expected rental increase, including the date.
- Everything that's included or excluded in the rent, such as utilities, parking, or storage.

Sometimes, a lease may also be referred to as a rental contract. Although very similar to lease agreements, there is a difference when it comes to rental contracts; it's all about the duration of the agreement. Generally, a rental agreement spans over a shorter period, usually 30 days. They are more flexible, allowing you or the landlord to terminate the agreement at the end of each month.

If the initial contract with your rental lease agreement is not renegotiated, it simply carries over to the next month until you give notice. On the other hand, lease agreements tend to be more long-term. It's a binding agreement between a landlord and a tenant, usually lasting for a year or more. It's great as it offers security! However, breach the contract and you may kiss your deposit goodbye. Plus, the landlord can sue you as well, landing you in a legal tango.

What Documents Do You Need?

Once you've found your perfect abode, you'll need to be approved by your leasing agent or landlord. Here's how to put your best foot forward:

- You need at least the last three months' pay stubs.
- You need to have held your current job for at least six months.

- You might be required to supply your bank records to show what balances you carry.
- You should be earning three to three and a half times the rent amount each month.
- You'll need some references, both professional and personal, to vouch that you're responsible.
- Of course, there might be an additional fee charged to run your credit reports, especially if you're a first-timer.

What Are the Rules?

There are rules and rights for everything in life and the relationship between a tenant and their landlord is no exception. Here's a quick rundown of some fundamental rules:

Tenant Rights	Landlord Duties
Protected from housing discrimination by the Fair Housing Act	Perform essential maintenance and repairs
Privacy rights within the rented premises	Maintain shared spaces
Right to peaceful living	Maintain the condition of the rental property
Right to secure, comfortable, and habitable conditions	Give advance notice before entering
Right to a residence that is devoid of lead poisoning and mold	Reimburse the security deposit within the required time frame set by law
	Follow eviction procedures outlined in local and state laws
	Inform the tenant if the property faces foreclosure
	Give a written notice of eviction
	Adhere to the legal process for eviction
	Cover legal fees if the landlord wins the eviction case

Rental Insurance

Any clue about what rental insurance is? It's pretty simple; rental insurance is a policy that acts as a safety buffer for your personal belongings when misfortune strikes.

It covers things like electronics, clothes, furniture, and a whole lot of other items. So, if something out of the ordinary like a fire, theft, vandalism, or water damage happens, your insurance helps cover the replacement (actual cash value coverage) or repair (replacement cost coverage) costs.

Renter's insurance also covers liability. This means that when someone gets injured in your place or on the property and you're accountable, your insurance can swoop in and contribute to the medical bills and legal fees. Keep in mind that rental insurance is not a financial floodgate. The payouts are all dependent on the type of loss and your amount of coverage. The costs vary depending on various factors, such as where you live and how much coverage you need. However, it's usually pretty affordable considering the peace of mind it buys you.

The big question: Do you really need it? It's not required by law, but a lot of lease agreements may insist on having rental insurance. But, even if they don't, it's a smooth move to protect you against the unexpected.

HANDS-ON ELEMENT: CREATE YOUR PERSONAL BUDGET PLAN

Now that you've picked up the fundamentals and a couple of strategies for budgeting, it's time to put your knowledge into practice and create your very own budget plan!

Simply stick to the following guidelines:

1. Gather and assess

A. Get all your financial statements together, from income sources like allowances and part-time jobs to expenses, such as subscriptions and personal purchases.

B. Categorize your expenses into "needs," which will include essentials such as transportation, and "wants," which are all the non-essentials that you can cut back on.

2. Define your goals

A. Draw up a list of your short-term and long-term financial goals.

B. Whether it's a new laptop or saving for college, make sure they're SMART (Specific, Measurable, Achievable, Relevant, Time-bound).

3. Make a budget template

A. Use a spreadsheet or budgeting app to create your budget template.

B. Allocate your income, prioritizing your "needs" first, followed by your financial goals, and finally, your "wants."

4. Track your spending

A. Keep an eye on those spending habits and record both income and expenses in your budget template.

B. After a month, review your template to identify areas where you can tweak and reduce unnecessary spending.

5. Review and reflect

A. Remember, budgets are dynamic! Regularly review your budget and make the necessary changes to ensure that you stay aligned with your financial goals.

Becoming a master with your finances does take time and effort, but it will most certainly pay off significantly in the long run. Remember, the more you practice, the better you'll become. So, stick to your plan, and keep refining it to see your goals materialize.

Now that we've wrapped up the fundamentals of finance, you're well on your way to mastering budgeting, and navigating savings, investments, loans, and credit cards. Hey, you can even move into your own place!

But, there's one thing missing. How will you sustain yourself? I suppose you need a career path, right?

Let's take a look at how you can make informed career choices that best align with your interests and values.

CHAPTER TWO

CAREER PATH FINDING

When it comes to career possibilities, life's a maze out there! What would you choose? Most importantly, why would you choose that specific career?

Each turn pops out a new possibility, another opportunity, another challenge, and a whole bunch of questions to fry your mind. Finding the perfect fit for your career isn't just about the paycheck; it's about doing something you love, something that aligns with your values and interests. It shouldn't only be the perfect fit; it should inspire you at the same time. After all, on average, a person spends a total of nine waking hours per day working. And, this is not exactly something that should be taken lightly.

You should not just be asking yourself "What will pay the bills?" but also, "What sets my soul on fire?" When you find that sweet spot where your skills, values, and interests intersect, magic happens. You need to wake up with a sense of purpose every day, knowing that you're not just punching a time clock, but you're also contributing to something meaningful and fulfilling.

So, why not hunt down your passion, do what you love, and get paid for it?

CHOOSING YOUR PATH

I am sure, as a teen, you're tired of the question "What do you want to do with your life?" It's a valid question though, and it's never too early to ponder and explore your options. But, where do you start?

The great news is that there are plenty of places you can start! Let's get the ball rolling with a few helpful pointers to steer you in the right direction:

- Kick-off with a bit of self-discovery and do an aptitude (to identify where your skills excel) and personality (to reveal your strengths and preferences) test.
- Make a list of potential careers that pique your interest along with reasons why they intrigue you.
- Delve into the world of these careers, looking at important aspects such as required qualifications, average salaries, industry trends, and growth forecasts to gauge future demand. A great source to gain some insights is the U.S. Bureau of Labor Statistics.
- Get out there and connect with experienced professionals in your fields of interest to gain more insight. You can even take it a step further and ask for a shadowing or intern position to get hands-on experience and a firsthand look at what each career entails.
- Start aligning your school work and additional studies with your interests. Research colleges and programs that will best facilitate and align with your goals. Explore all your options, even alternative routes such as trade programs and entrepreneurship.

- Don't forget to enlist the expertise of high school counselors. They're your guides in career planning, scholarship opportunities, and preparing for the exciting road ahead.

Values, Passion, and Pressure

Sure, you need to choose a career path that's aligned with your passions and values! Piece of cake, right? Let me ask you, though, what's your purpose?

To fulfill your purpose, you need a solid plan that gives you direction and meaning. So, direction is guided by your values, and meaning is provided by your passions.

The best place to start would be to identify your values because this will serve as your career aspirations' foundation. Reflect on what truly matters to you in life to help define your values. Once you pinpointed your values, be sure that the decisions you make and the actions you take align with these values, leading to greater fulfillment and authenticity. Up next, it's all about passion!

To discover your passions, simply think of all the things you do that bring you pure joy, the things that make you lose track of time. Additionally, identify your strengths and areas in which you excel. Don't hold back, prioritize and embrace your passions. When you discover what brings you true joy and understand your values, you'll discover a deeper sense of existence, and this is what is called your purpose! And, when you have a purpose, you have a strong guiding force that will prioritize your goals over short-term gains.

Now, at times, the passion lines may get blurred due to external pressures and expectations nudging you toward more "profitable" options. This most certainly can feel somewhat suffocating, and confusing, even causing serious health problems such as depression and anxiety. But, what are your motives? Are you just stirring the pot to rebel or are you truly sticking to what you believe in?

Here are a couple of tips to help you stay true to your passion-filled path:

- What activities make time fly by effortlessly? This is a good indicator of passion.
- Write down your top ten qualities to gain more insight into your strengths.
- Take those personality and aptitude tests for a deeper awareness of your strengths and interests.
- Hit up a couple of free online career quizzes.
- Represent yourself effectively and journal about your personality, skills, and experiences to reflect on and keep track of your development over time. You might just spot a pattern or two!

People might have your best interests at heart with their suggestions, however, it's your life's journey and you have to take responsibility for your decisions. Stay open to possibilities, but always stick to your values.

Here are a few straightforward tactics to help you deal with societal and familial pressure:

- **Put it into perspective:** Others' opinions are, well, just that—their opinions. People differ, and that's great! Their expectations do not necessarily reflect your capabilities or align with your values. Understanding this little golden truth will enable you to ease some of the unrealistic pressure off yourself.

- **What are your expectations?** What are some of the expectations you have for others? If you can understand your own motives, it will grant you more insight into why you respond the way you do to external pressures.
- **Follow your gut:** Make sure to regularly spend time reflecting on yourself to discover and better understand your desires and goals. As mentioned, write it down to help spot what truly matters to you beyond any external factors, whether it be influences, pressures, or rewards.
- **Be assertive:** Be sure to voice your needs in a respectful, constructive manner. Your preferences do matter and you are deserving of living your best life.

TACKLING CAREER UNCERTAINTY

We all find ourselves feeling a little lost in life at times, and it may feel rather disheartening. Yet, it's life nudging you to get out of your comfort zone and explore new horizons. Sure, change may be uncomfortable because we fear the unknown, but change is inevitable. What you need is a good plan with a good strategy.

Let's outline the components of an effective strategy for achieving your career goals:

- **How would you know what you want to do if you're not sure what's out there?** As mentioned, research various career options, considering all the fundamentals such as qualifications and skills required, and advancement opportunities to name a few.
- **Without a goal, you might end up in circles.** Set specific short and long-term goals, targeting a bull's eye for actions taken in the next three to five years. Make sure that the goals are centered around skill development and gaining

experience toward your desired career options. Remember to be SMART with your goals for an effective action plan!

- **You're an explorer and you won't have all the answers.** Thus, be flexible in your approaches to bring about changes that will benefit you. It's all about learning and expanding as a person.
- **Measure your progress and celebrate your wins.** Even the small ones! Yes, every drop adds up and contributes to a full bucket, enabling you to overflow with confidence and more certainty.
- **Keep track of your progress.** Document your goals, challenges, and achievements to help you keep track of progress and where changes can be made for improvement.

Exploring Careers

A great prepping strategy for your career is to get on board with an internship that will enable you to build some good skills and open you up to real-world experiences. Think of it as a bit of a head start.

It's not about landing your dream job, but rather, an internship, and is all about learning and growing, granting you time to best figure things out as you go along. Internships are a great way to pinpoint what you want to or don't want to learn and get better at. One of the best perks of an internship is that you get to have a mentor who can give you guidance and feedback.

Here's a summary of why you should go for an internship and find yourself a good mentor:

- You get real-world hands-on experience.
- You get to explore different career paths.

- Internships on your resume set you apart from other candidates for future employers.
- You get guidance from experienced professionals in your chosen field.
- Hey, some internships even pay you.
- You get to expand your network, opening yourself up to more opportunities.
- You can try out new things.
- Some internships may even lead to full-time employment!

Landing Your Internship

Getting an internship is going to require a bit of know-how from your side, however, it's completely doable. Here are a couple of pointers:

- Know what you want first of all. This will make it easier to narrow down the options you should focus on.
- Tap into your network, letting friends, family, and teachers know that you're on the lookout for an internship.
- Hop online and dive into the tons of platforms and websites, such as Indeed, Internships.com, and LinkedIn, to hunt for internships.
- Many schools have internship programs and resources to help students find internships. Be sure to check in and find out what your options are.
- Dress to impress and attend job fairs to network and get into contact with potential employers.
- You will need a resume when applying for an internship. Be sure that it's tailored to the specific position you're applying for, highlighting all your relevant skills in that field.

- Always follow up after applying or going for an internship interview. It will help you show interest and stand out from the crowd.

Don't feel discouraged along the way. Rejection and setbacks are all part of the package, the right opportunity will eventually come knocking.

Reviving Evolving Career Paths

Life carries on, you evolve, and it shouldn't come as a surprise if you have felt the urge to change course in your career. It's rather common.

There are many reasons for this "nudge," such as the need for a fresh challenge, wanting a more balanced work-life, or simply continuing to follow your passion. One piece of advice—don't just blindly dive in and make the shift. Some self-reflection and evaluation are highly recommended. You need to reassess your interests and talents because they may change as you evolve, revealing promising new paths. As with everything, strategy comes into play when you want to shine a light on potential roles' realities.

For an effective career shift consider the following strategy:

- Assess your current situation, considering why you want the change and how feasible it will be.
- Re-evaluate your passions and abilities to explore different options that may align more with your interests and skills.
- As always, do your homework and research the relevant industries' roles and job markets, searching online and networking.
- When you find an available open position, update your resume, network profiles, and necessary skills.

- Ready yourself for some possible challenges, such as longer job search periods that will require more sacrifices.
- Remember, keep track of your progress, applications, and feedback to help keep you motivated.

Charting a new career course with commitment may lead to more fulfilling outcomes:

- greater job satisfaction
- increased earning potential
- a greater sense of meaning and fulfillment
- improved overall well-being

Always trust your inner compass and follow your guiding star. It may take some courage to change courses, but if the rewards are worth it, why not?

RESUME BUILDING

Now, we've been talking about a resume and making sure it's suited for the application you're interested in. I'm sure you know what it entails, however, there are some fine details besides your personal info, education, and job experience that need some good thought.

A catchy resume should be easy to digest at a glance. Think about it: How many resumes do recruiters have to scan through and what's going to make you stand out?

Be sure to include the following eight key sections:

Basics

- **Personal info:** This will include your name and all relevant contact information, including relevant social network profiles. However, your home address may not be required.
- **Summary:** Write a short, convincing summary that will show why you're the perfect fit for the job. With so many AI writing tools available, you wouldn't have to think long and hard about it compared to ten years ago.
- **Education:** List your highest level of education, including impressive achievements such as rewards or scholarships.
- **Experience:** This is always a "biggie." List your relevant work experiences and be sure to highlight your skills and achievements that align with the job you're applying for.
- **Skills:** List both your hard (technical or job-specific skills that are acquired through training or experience) and soft skills (how you interact with others; attributes such as communication, teamwork, problem-solving, and time management). A lovely little tip: Use phrases from the job posting to pass automated reviews!
- **Certifications:** Include any certifications that boost and solidify your qualifications.
- **References:** If you're a bit short on experience, include references of educators or networking companions.
- **Other requirements:** Double check for any local-related expectations for resumes where you live or specific to your job application.

Design

- Keep your grid layout aligned and tidy.
- Leave some white space, avoiding cramming in information.
- Start with a template, there's plenty on the internet to choose from, and simply save it as a PDF to keep the formatting intact.
- Use different font sizes and colors to make key information stand out. But, only stick to three simple colors max, it's not a coloring book.
- Keep it simple when it comes to fonts, making use of basics such as Open Sans or Roboto.
- Create a personal logo for an extra polished look.
- incorporate subtle details like icons or illustrations for some added personality.
- If you're not applying for a job in a creative field, it's best to keep it clean and simple.

See? Easy as pie!

Acquiring Relevant Skills and Experience

Change is indeed inevitable, but so is the process of learning in life. After all, that's what change is all about, right? You can either go about it the hard way or simply take it in your stride.

Learning new skills is pivotal for career development, as it can lead you down paths you may not have previously considered. It's crucial to progress, take on fresh projects, and use your knowledge to stay ahead in the game. Most importantly, an attitude that reflects a willingness to learn will showcase not only your commitment but also your value as a person.

For a speedy ascent up the career ladder, harness the following steps:

- Set clear learning goals for what you want to achieve.
- Break your skill set down into smaller, separate sub-skills to make the process attainable and keep you as motivated as a player in a high-stakes boss battle.
- Start with one sub-skill set and create an actionable plan, identifying any potential challenges or barriers to determine how you can make your development more realistic and accessible. Only focus on one new sub-skill at a time, as you don't want to feel overwhelmed.
- Fully embrace the 80/20 rule, which suggests that 20% of learning approaches can lead to accomplishing 80% of your goal.
- Learning a new skill is a form of personal development, and you will have to dedicate some time to engage in this practice and hone your skills. Thus, prioritize your personal development, as every step contributes to giant leaps in your future.
- Learning new skills doesn't happen overnight. So, you should get comfortable with setting more long-term goals and breaking them down into smaller, short-term goals that will help you stay focused and monitor your progress effectively.
- Seek opportunities and additional resources to learn and polish your skills:

  - Go online to access resources and network with professionals.
  - Stay up to date and learn about the latest technology and industry trends.

○ Dive into books and case studies to be more informed about the facts.

○ Develop skills that are in demand in the job market.

○ Improve both hard and soft skills to be well-rounded.

○ Consider enrolling in professional development courses.

○ Get out there and attend professional events such as conferences or talks.

○ Whether it's a role model or a mentor, learn from others.

○ Making mistakes is not the end of the world, as long as you learn from them. They're some of life's greatest teachers, often misunderstood as punishments instead of tools for learning.

Your Talent Show!

The job market is a competitive "sport," making it both an art and a science to stand out from the crowd. It's more than just tossing your resume into the ring; it's all about highlighting your skills and experiences and making hiring managers and recruiters do a double-take.

Let's take a look at how you can make an unforgettable first impression:

- Be creative and specific with your headings. Use a header such as "Marketing Experience" instead of the generic "Work History" to make recruiters do a double take.
- Pepper your resume with industry-specific buzzwords and terminology to show your competency.
- Let your achievements do the talking and weave through some testimonial quotes from evaluations and recommendations to add some extra social proof.

- Actions speak louder than words! Include concrete examples, like publications and online portfolios, that showcase your skills and accomplishments.
- If you want to impress them even more, do a bit of research on the company you're applying to and see where and how you can improve and contribute to their existing structure. Act like an expert and share insights related to the specific industry. This will directly showcase your value and problem-solving abilities.
- Take it a step further by bringing your resume to life, and create a video resume to showcase your skills in a more personal, dynamic way.
- Engage in side projects that will showcase your passion and dedication in the relevant market.

HANDS-ON ELEMENT: DEVELOP YOUR PERSONAL CAREER EXPLORATION PLAN

Time to put all your career planning prowess to practice! It's time to shine the light on developing your personal career exploration plan that aligns with your values, interests, aspirations, and strengths.

1. **Discover your passion:** Start by doing a self-assessment. Grab your journal and jot down all the activities that make you lose track of time and do a few personality tests to help pinpoint your passion.
2. **Potential careers:** Next, list jobs that match your interests and strengths. Get the inside scoop on each job, researching what they involve, the qualifications required, and the future job market outlook.
3. **Internship:** Reach out to experienced people in the

relevant fields, securing an internship or a mentor to gain hands-on experience and test the waters.

4. **Set goals:** Set both short-term and long-term goals based on your research. Short-term goals could include joining online classes or workshops related to your interests, while long-term goals may involve pursuing specific degrees or applying for starter jobs.

5. **Create a map:** Map out the steps for each goal. Remember the SMART goal method! This will help you establish a realistic strategy for success.

6. **Take action:** A dream will merely be wishful thinking without action. Take small steps toward your goals every day. And, remember, it's all about consistency and perseverance.

7. **Review:** Review your progress regularly and bring forth changes where necessary. Reach out for support from family, friends, educators, and mentors for guidance and motivation.

Most importantly, you need to be flexible in your approaches. You're on a journey of self-discovery, so be willing to learn and adapt as you go.

What's more essential than the latest TikTok trends? Relationships! Yes, building meaningful relationships in both your personal and professional life is a true fine art that's well worth mastering. So, let's huddle along and look at the secrets of building meaningful connections that will enrich your life.

CHAPTER THREE

FOSTERING RELATIONSHIPS

Here's the thing: Not all relationships are created equal. Some lift your spirits and others, well, they drag you down. You know those gossip-loving, drama-spreading Fairweather Friends that disappear the second things get real? Energy vampires!

Nobody should make time for that kind of negativity, life's too short and there's too much to do. What you need are "ride-or-dies" who have your back no matter what. The genuine folks that build you up when you feel down, make you laugh when you cry, and would gladly step in if anyone disrespects you. Surrounding yourself with positive people pays off in the long run. Healthy relationships reduce anxiety and stress while boosting self-confidence. And, they're just a whole lot more fun!

Your time is precious and you're valuable, so be picky about who you spend your time with. Let's take a closer look at why and how you can trade in the fakes for ones who share your values.

UNDERSTANDING EFFECTIVE COMMUNICATION

Communicating effectively is not just about getting things off your chest. It's multifaceted, involving various aspects, such as speaking clearly, ensuring your needs are understood, and listening attentively—all while maintaining empathy throughout.

Empathy

It's all about tuning in and truly understanding where others come from. You need to wrap your mind and ears in empathy and have the ability to walk a mile in another person's shoes.

- **Actively listen:** We all hear people when they talk, but how many times do we truly listen? Active listening means you tune in to what someone is saying, trying to sincerely understand their perspective and emotions.
- **Respond:** When people open up to you, keep an open mind, acknowledging and validating their experiences. Respond empathetically by making use of statements such as "I see why you feel this way," or "What you went through sounds tough."
- **Ask:** A power move in effective communication is to ask empathetic questions that show genuine interest and curiosity. Keep the questions open-ended such as "Why did it make you feel that way?" or "Tell me more about what happened," to clarify and gain a deeper understanding of their perspective.
- **Timing:** Timing is everything! Respond to concerns promptly, especially when the stakes are high. Nobody likes being kept out of the loop. Remember, communication is a two-way street, so give them space to respond without jumping in to fill the silence.

- **Wording:** Choose your words carefully, avoiding insincere clichés. Also, watch that tone. A lot of the time is not what we say, but rather how we say it.

Being able to engage in a constructive, empathetic conversation creates an environment of inclusivity and mutual respect, the fundamental building blocks of healthy, fulfilling relationships.

The ABCs of Clear Communication

We all love a good hack, right? And there's, indeed, a good one when it comes to clear, empathetic communication: the ABCs!

It's all about accuracy, brevity, and clarity. And, here's how to nail it:

Accuracy

- Understand your audience to structure your message and words accordingly.
- Always be sure that your message is free from bias and factual, ensuring inclusivity.
- When writing, be sure to check your grammar, punctuation, and spelling!

Brevity

- Keep your messages short and sweet. They should be concise and straight to the point to maintain audience engagement.
- There is power in silence. Know when to speak and when to be quiet, granting others the opportunity to voice their thoughts.
- Listen actively and invite feedback for open communication.

Clarity

- Avoid flowery expressions and be overly descriptive to enhance understanding.
- Keep your message straightforward, logical, well-articulated, and free from ambiguity to elicit clear responses.

Verbal and Nonverbal Cues

The multifaceted nature of communication may come across as somewhat puzzling, especially if you throw human emotion into the mix. But, with a solid understanding of the fundamentals, you'll be well on track to becoming a smooth talker and a great listener.

For now, let's hone in on listening and non-verbal communication to paint a clearer picture.

Listening

There are five different levels of listening according to Stephen R. Covey, author of *The 7 Habits of Highly Effective People* (Wilson, 2021):

- ignoring someone
- pretending to listen to someone
- selective hearing
- attentive listening
- empathic listening

Attenuative and empathic listening are the two you want to check. However, when it comes to the king of the ring, empathic listening takes the crown because this is when you try to understand others first before expressing your own thoughts and opinions. It's a very powerful form of listening, where trust and humility have to be established. However, if you understand the four stages of empathic listening, you'll be a great listener in the blink of an eye:

- **Mimicking:** This is the first stage, which is generally taught in active listening courses.
- **Rephrasing:** Rephrasing what someone said is effective but still limited when it comes to the verbal part of communication.
- **Reflecting:** The stage of reflecting the speaker's feelings, in addition to their words, sets the stage for the grand finale.
- **Rephrasing and reflecting:** Offer the speaker a breath of psychological fresh air, merging stages 2 and 3 seamlessly.

Nonverbal Communication

Nonverbal communication refers to your body language. Surprisingly, these messages may come across as stronger compared to verbal communication. Yes, your body language can speak more than words!

Nonverbal cues include your facial expressions, posture, gestures, body movement, eye contact, voice, touch, and space. You can immediately see if someone isn't happy with what is being said just by their facial expression, or imagine an excited person's tone of voice and hands explaining something to you.

- **Facial expression:** Whether it's expressing surprise, fear, joy, anger, or disgust, the human face is a powerful tool. These expressions are universal, transcending cultural boundaries.
- **Posture and body movement:** Your thoughts and feelings flow forth from the way you carry yourself. The way you

walk, talk, sit, and so much more influences the perceptions of others.

- **Gestures:** Gestures are actions that help you convey messages without words. Be wary though, as they differ across cultures.
- **Eye contact:** Ah, the windows to your soul, signaling affection, attraction, and hostility. Your eyes are a dead giveaway to gauge response and level of engagement.
- **Voice:** The tone, timing, and inflection of your voice all add an extra layer to the meaning and intention of your message.
- **Touch:** Touch carries so much intention and emotion. From a handshake to a hug, touch is one of the most powerful forms of nonverbal communication.
- **Space:** Your personal space also influences communication, gauging intimacy, affection, aggression, or dominance.

It's very important to be aware of not only body language but also cultural differences when it comes to the correct interpretation of cues to avoid any misunderstandings. As you can see, communication is more than just talking. Your body communicates through various functions, including repetition, contradiction, substitution, complementing, and accenting. Indeed, actions speak louder than words!

Along with verbal communication, nonverbal communication plays a very important role when it comes to conveying messages, and empathic listening is pivotal when it comes to understanding perspective. All three aspects contribute to effective communication that fosters understanding and connection between people.

Common Communication Barriers

Communication does come with challenges, but there are some great tactics you can employ to overcome them.

Here's a quick rundown of challenges and strategies to pivot conversations in a healthier direction:

Listening

Physical discomfort or ailment: If you're not feeling in tip-top shape, you're not going to be able to pay full attention.

- **Tip:** Reschedule the conversation.

Being critical: Being judgmental and subjective toward the speaker.

- **Tip:** Focus on the message, not the messenger to maintain an objective stance.

Preoccupation: When you're thinking ahead of your next response.

- **Tip:** Consciously silence your inner voice and focus intently on the speaker, honing in on their verbal and nonverbal cues.

Information overload: Too much information can make it rather confusing and overbearing to stay focused.

- **Tip:** Try to hone in on the relevant points of the conversation.

Intense emotional reactions: Experiencing intense emotional reactions as a response.

- **Tip:** Ground yourself and make a conscious effort to not be overwhelmed by your emotions. Remember to focus on the facts and be objective.

External disturbances: External distractions such as noise, phones, or extreme temperatures can be bothersome.

- **Tip:** Minimize distractions or change locations.

In a nutshell, for effective listening:

- pause
- pay attention
- listen
- have empathy
- be inquisitive
- rephrase

Perception

Neglecting to invest time: Misconceptions caused by overlooking details and making assumptions.

- **Tip:** Situations are complex, and sometimes they need a bit more of your time to hone in on the details. Do some investigation before drawing conclusions.

Generalizing and categorizing: When you stereotype and generalize based on preconceptions.

- **Tip:** Never judge a book by its cover. Always grant a person time to express themselves. Remember, nobody's entirety is defined by one moment.

Experiencing inconsistency: When words and body language don't coincide, it can not only be confusing but also come across as unreliable.

- **Tip:** Be consistent with your actions and words, making sure they align. If you find the speaker is inconsistent, simply ask for clarification.

Negativity bias: Human nature tends to lean more toward the negatives than the positives. Thus, a lot of the time the negatives will stand out, leaving you to completely overlook the positives.

- **Tip:** Remember, a story is multifaceted, consisting of both positives and negatives. Don't let negative comments or statements overshadow the positives. Sure, take note, but don't judge.

Assuming agreement: Not everyone interprets things the same way, and this could lead to misunderstanding.

- **Tip:** Understand everyone is entitled to their own opinions. Allow others theirs while being sure to assert yours respectfully.

In a nutshell, for effective perception:

- Ask for feedback from others.
- Focus on comprehending others.
- Scrutinize personal perceptions.

Verbal Communication

Self-doubt: Low self-esteem, shyness, and low self-worth prevent you from getting your needs met and opinions heard.

- **Tip:** Be aware that *you matter* and so do your needs and opinions. Recognize that you have a right to freely and respectfully express yourself, just like everyone else.

Unclarity: Vague wording, or making use of overly formal language can obscure the "moral of the story."

- **Tip:** Communication is not about impressing people; it's about getting a message across and having your needs understood. Be clear and concise, steering clear of any jargon.

Rushing to conclusions: Confusing facts with tendencies.

- **Tip:** Measure the facts against your own insights you attach to the situation with an open mind.

Referencing stereotypes and generalizing: Undermine your own intelligence by making assumptions and being judgmental.

- **Tip:** Stick to the facts and be objective, avoiding extremes and always showcasing empathy.

Ineffective responses: Responding too quickly, interrupting, being irrelevant, or ignoring a question leads to poor communication.

- **Tip:** Be patient with others and yourself. Pause before you answer, and if you're unsure, ask for a moment and say you'll revert back.

In a nutshell, for effective verbal communication:

- employ supportive responses
- embrace authenticity
- acknowledge your worth and experiences
- demonstrate empathy
- embrace adaptability and open-mindedness

PRACTICAL COMMUNICATION STRATEGIES

Expressing yourself effectively isn't just about getting others to listen—it's also about earning their respect. You're assertive, yet warm. You know how to get a story across, field through questions, and, most importantly, when to say "no."

It's not something you're either born with or not, it's just a few simple tricks of the trade. Here we go:

- **Reflect on previous interactions.** Take some time to reflect on past experiences, analyzing your emotions to identify any recurring patterns to better grasp your emotional responses.
- **Always put yourself in another person's shoes to better understand their perspective.** You never know what

someone else has been through and how it impacted them. Be cautious of judgment.

- **Conversations, especially heated discussions, are not about winning or losing.** Focus on solutions, trying to find a level ground that benefits everyone involved.
- **Recognize that your thoughts and opinions matter.** If those nerves kick in, simply focus on your positive traits and accomplishments for a confidence boost.
- **Overthinking kills creativity!** Relax and be yourself. Those who truly appreciate you will not be concerned about judging you, and those who judge you don't deserve your concern.
- **Maintain eye contact to personalize the conversation and use open body language to appear confident and approachable.** Last but not least, flash that beautiful smile, it's attractive!
- **Negative assumptions can be extremely overwhelming.** Refuse to let them swallow you whole and evaluate where they sprung from objectively to curb social anxiety.
- **Avoid filler words.** "Um, like, um." That's vague and reeks of insecurity. Practice speaking without filler words. You can record yourself or ask for feedback to improve in this area.
- **Sharing is caring, but some things are best left to the imagination.** Avoid oversharing information. Find a balance between being open and appropriate in social interactions.
- **Keep it simple.** It's fantastic if you have a great vocabulary; however, it might not always be the best move to fling around your "supercalifragilisticexpialidocious" words because it might confuse or alienate others. If you are communicating complex ideas, speak clearly and use simple, understandable words.

- **Don't take things personally.** You don't have to internalize and assume personal responsibility for others' behaviors. You can only control yourself, let go of what you can't control.
- **Try coaching for extra help.** Consider working with a social skills coach for personalized guidance and accountability.

Adapting Your Communication Style

Adapting your conversation style is important to be able to juggle the conversation jungle out there, and flexibility is your vine! This is very important when it comes to communicating your intended message effectively across different audiences. Let's take a look at some tricks of the trade:

- **Understand your audience:** Know who you're talking to. There's a big difference when you communicate with your boss, at a meeting, or with your friends. Understand the crowd and the appropriate cues and tailor your communication to suit their preferences.
- **What's your objective?** What's the purpose of the conversation and what results are you aiming for? Anticipate reactions and adjust your tone, tweaking your message accordingly to achieve your goals.
- **Continuously monitor:** Engage in active listening and keep an eye on the people's responses and body cues during your conversation to gauge whether you should bring about some changes to your communication style as needed to ensure clarity.
- **Stay flexible:** This is probably one of the most important points: staying flexible. You need to know when and how to pivot smoothly to keep your audience hooked. Be

prepared to adjust your approach as the situation demands.

- **"Feel, Felt, Found" method:** Acknowledge your audience's feelings by empathizing and mirroring their cues. Relate by sharing similar experiences. Offer objective solutions and insights to address concerns.
- **Ask for feedback:** Solicit feedback from your audience to gain a better understanding of whether your communication style resonated or not. Use this feedback to refine your approach and improve future interactions.
- **Keep it real:** Adapting your communication style doesn't mean you have to sell yourself short. Stay authentic, staying true to yourself and your values will help build trust and credibility with your audience.

Managing Tough Talks

Awkward conversations and disagreements are an inevitable part of any relationship. However, there are healthy, constructive ways to manage these difficult discussions and resolve these awkward, challenging moments.

The key is to approach it with understanding, empathy, and a solutions-focused mindset. There are often three layers to these conversations: the facts, the emotions, and deeper issues of identity. Taking time to get clear on each layer can help prevent you from getting overwhelmed or reactive. Evaluate the issue, keeping the end goal in mind: a resolution that works for all parties involved. When you make the solution about finding an option that addresses everyone's needs, you're guaranteed a more positive outcome.

Instead of attacking or blaming, which isn't constructive, it helps to come from a place of curiosity, sharing your own experiences.

This will show interest and that you can resonate with the other person. Choosing the right time and place, when emotions are calm, can make a big difference. Thus, when things get heated, try stepping away for a moment and waiting for the dust to settle.

And, prevention is better than a cure! Thus, building a character that shouts trust and psychological safety will create a perception that you are approachable. This, in turn, creates an environment where difficult conversations don't escalate into full-blown conflicts.

Active listening, compassionate communication, and encouraging feedback are your superpowers during these awkward talks. And, hey, with these in the mix, awkward moments become opportunities for growth and stronger bonds.

BUILDING STRONGER CONNECTIONS THROUGH COMMUNICATION

Communication is a two-way street where ideas, feelings, and information are exchanged. It's all fun and games if all parties involved understand each other clearly.

This means that there has to be understanding, trust, cooperation, and respect. Striving for these communication goals isn't just a noble pursuit, they directly influence the quality of your life. And, here's how proper communication improves not only your quality of life but those of others as well:

- Effective communication makes people feel understood and heard because it fosters validation.
- When communication is open and honest it means people are sharing their thoughts and feelings authentically. This

  vulnerability and intimacy create a foundation of trust
    within relationships.
  • When you engage in active listening, empathy, and
    validation, you establish deeper emotional connections.
  • Effective communication is a powerful tool to clear the air
    around conflicts and misunderstandings, allowing for
    stronger bonds and better understanding between people.

Words have power and, as you can see, they play an important part when it comes to building healthy meaningful relationships. It's like your little "abracadabra" to stir up connection and understanding. So, choose your words wisely!

Communication, Trust, and Understanding

Words are like bricks that construct the foundations of healthy relationships. If you're a master builder and you know how to lay and plaster those nouns, verbs, and everything in between, you'll be constructing a beautiful village of love and support that could weather any storm.

As with building a sturdy abode, there's a strategy involved in constructing these strong bonds, one of which is to make time for others. Hit the brakes and take time out to fill up your relationship tanks with some "talk time." This will not only keep you in touch with what's happening in the lives of those you care for but also make them feel loved and validated. But, when you do so, be sure that you're there listening more than you're talking. This sincere move on your part will grant you a deeper insight and understanding of a person. Hey, you're not a mind-reader, so ask questions and steer clear of assumptions, getting first-hand information straight from the "horse's mouth" to eliminate any misunderstandings during your interactions.

After all, communication is an exchange, not a blame game or crit session. Keep it positive and constructive. You're part of a verbal team, not an opponent in a debate. Own your feelings by making use of "I" statements to express yourself without unnecessary drama while paying attention to your tone of voice. Remember, it's not just about what you say, but how you say it.

Understand what makes the other person happy to bring some extra, thoughtful sunshine and joy. Relationships are not just there as a shoulder to cry on; they're supposed to improve and uplift. It's an art of giving and taking, not winning or losing.

And, if you need to take a break from a situation or a person, do so with respect and empathy. It's better to grant yourself some space and a chance to recharge, enabling you to come back stronger.

Power Up Your EQ

You're very well aware of IQ, your intelligence quotient, right? But, what about EQ?

EQ is your emotional intelligence, which refers to understanding and managing both your own emotions and those of others. So, what exactly makes someone emotionally intelligent?

Well, it starts with self-awareness, recognizing and understanding your own emotional states that enable you to navigate the complexities of human interactions with graceful authenticity. Then, there's a good dose of self-regulation coupled with this, which demonstrates restraint and thoughtfulness. This is the ability to keep your cool even in challenging situations.

However, it's not all just about managing your own emotions; it's also about your ability to tune into the emotions and perspectives of others. Yet again, this is where empathy kicks in, encompassing empathetic listening and social cues to really get where others are coming from.

Brushing up on your emotional intelligence is more than just mastering the art of emojis. Let's look at some savvy tips to improve this form of smarts:

- **Increase your self-awareness:** Engage in regular self-reflection to better understand your own emotions and reactions.
- **Recognize others' emotions:** Ask some trusted people how they perceive your behavior and why. You can learn a lot from a different perspective.
- **Be an active listener:** You know the drill; don't only listen to what's said but also keep your eyes peeled on the subtleties such as emotional cues.
- **Be clear:** Communicate clearly and respectfully to deliver your message and set clear expectations and vice versa.
- **Keep an open mind:** Empathy is the key to an open mind that will help you acknowledge and respect new ideas and perspectives. This opens you up to new possibilities and makes you more approachable.
- **Stay positive:** This might be easier said than done, but maintaining a calm, positive attitude and focusing on solutions during tough talks will lessen the sting of a confrontation, encouraging a more supportive environment where everyone is acknowledged and respected.
- **Accept feedback:** Be open to feedback; however, be aware that not all feedback is dished out as a constructive opportunity for growth and improvement. Be honest, take what resonates, and discard any irrelevant comments.

Life's too short for extra baggage filled with unnecessary tainted opinions.

HANDS-ON ELEMENT: ENHANCE YOUR COMMUNICATION SKILLS

The goal of this hands-on exercise is to practice the nuances of effective communication to flex those communication skills, helping you foster stronger, more meaningful relationships.

1. Communication Check-Up

A. Self-reflect on your communication style and identify areas in need of improvement, whether it be active listening, emotional regulation, or clarity in expression. Are you a chatterbox or a good listener? Do you express yourself freely or do you tend to hold back? Keep those questions rolling to get a clear picture.

2. Conversational Bootcamp

A. Get out there and engage in conversations, focusing on different aspects such as active listening, clear communication, and getting a firm grasp on the nuances of body language. Don't forget the power of eye contact; don't freak out, it's just two eyeballs! Pay attention to your tone and try using "I" statements for crystal-clear expression.

3. Conflict Resolution

A. Think of a past conflict or sticky conversation. How was it handled?

B. Write down how and where the situation could have been tackled differently by employing the effective communication strategies you've learned in this chapter.

C. If you're feeling brave and it's possible, give it another shot with the person involved and test out your new strategies.

4. Additional Tips

A. Always be flexible and open to feedback that will help you refine your communication style.

B. Keep a journal of your experiences, jotting down what worked and what didn't, and adjust your approaches accordingly.

Listen to podcasts or join workshops to practice and improve your skills daily. Communication is a skill that improves with patience and practice!

Effective communication sprouts from empathy. This is important if you want to establish and build healthy, meaningful relationships. Brush up on your EQ; it's an investment that will enable you to cover various aspects like clarity, empathy, active listening, and understanding nonverbal cues, all essential components for effective communication.

Now that you're well on your way to becoming a confident, smooth-talking individual, we'll step it a notch up and dive into the fascinating world of personal growth and development. From learning to laugh at yourself to embracing feedback with open arms, we'll explore every nook and cranny to unlock your full potential and conquer the world!

CHAPTER FOUR

PERSONAL GROWTH AND DEVELOPMENT

The truth about this personal growth thing? It's a lifelong adventure, meaning it doesn't ever stop. It's just like a road trip—you set a destination and enjoy all the sights along the way.

Every experience, good and bad, is progress. They all help shape you into your wise, confident future self. It's not about being perfect either. Thank heavens, right? Think of it as collecting skills along the way that you can add to your toolbox.

With every year, you collect more understanding about relationships, handling stress, and standing up for yourself. Sure, you'll make mistakes but don't sweat it, just change course and keep moving. When you fall, be sure to fall forward. The detours and wrong turns are part of the ride and are all little lessons for you to gain some profound wisdom.

Who's in the driver's seat of your life? You are! So, soak up all the good "feels" and adventures. So, let's step into the version of yourself that tackles challenges with confidence, manages stress like a pro, and organizes life with ease.

CULTIVATING SELF-WORTH AND CONFIDENCE

There are so many "selves" out there such as self-worth, self-awareness, self-care, self-love, self-compassion, and self-confidence, to name a few. They're all equally important, but let's start slow and take a look at self-worth and self-confidence for a solid start.

Self-worth is about recognizing the value and respect you hold for yourself, irrespective of external factors, which include things like your achievements or validation from others. You know you deserve love, respect, and kindness, including from yourself! You understand that you're worthy and appreciate yourself just the way you are; freckles, speckles, pimples, and all. Yes, you matter because you exist.

Then, there's the infamous, often misinterpreted, self-confidence. It's not about who can shout the loudest, rock the most fabulous hair, or rack up the highest number of likes on social media. True self-confidence is an intrinsic thing that is built on self-worth, adding an assured faith in your abilities and judgment. You carry a firm belief in yourself and your capacity for growth, enabling you to handle whatever challenges come your way with assurance and resilience.

Why are these so important? Because your self-perception shapes your reality! Self-worth and self-confidence are two major players when it comes to your personal well-being, success, and fulfillment. When you understand your worth and feel confident, you are able to freely and boldly be your authentic self. You radiate positivity, attract opportunity, and live courageously. External validation? That's not on your radar because you make decisions based on and aligned with your own goals and values. Without these two crucial traits, your full potential will only be but a distant dream, your voice and needs will be drowned out by doubt, and your goals buried under the debris of fear.

You're not here to people-please and earn your worthiness through external validation. You exist to be the best version of yourself. So, let's take a closer look at how you can own your power to unlock your personal growth and success in all areas of life.

Boosting Self-Esteem and Confidence

We all want a healthy dose of self-esteem and confidence, but it's rather a complex concept, to be honest. Many things can influence your self-esteem, such as your upbringing and certain events you experience. A lot of people cultivate a negative perception of themselves and their abilities due to these experiences, leading to low self-esteem.

Let's look at pretensions, for instance, your goals, values, and the things you believe about your potential. If these are high and your achievements are low, then you may think you're a failure. This negatively impacts your self-esteem. On the other hand, if your pretensions are low and you succeed at something, you'll have a higher sense of achievement, thus, boosting your self-esteem.

Then, we have the adolescent years. Ah, bliss, isn't it? This period has a significant hand at play when it comes to self-esteem, where you compare yourself to others. You constantly evaluate how others see you and what they think about you. So many factors! What to do?

Just stick to the basic plan: being the captain of your own ship. Here are a couple of pointers to help you do just that:

- **Mindfulness mastery:** Practicing mindfulness grounds you in the present moment. This enables you to silence the negative chatter of self-doubt and focus on the here and the now, not the worries about the past or future.
- **Comparison combat:** Your uniqueness is your strength! Why even compare a one-of-a-kind to the rest? Embrace your distinctiveness.
- **Storyline switch-up:** You have the power to change your narrative any time you want. Examine the negative stories and beliefs you hold about yourself. Where do they come from? What triggers them? Why do they impact you the way they do? Understand them then kick them to the curb. Instead, celebrate your wins and strengths.
- **Exercise elation:** Get those endorphins flowing by engaging in some feel-good fitness activities. A brisk walk, a round of tennis with a good friend, or simply a little stretching routine will not only get your heart pumping but also lift your spirits and send your confidence soaring.
- **Rockstar revelry:** Channel your inner superstar by indulging in activities you excel in. Whether it's serving up a delectable dish, being a wizard with words, or a karaoke connoisseur, let your talents shine bright.
- **Volunteer ventures:** Spread the love and join a volunteer program in your free time to help others. This will not only make a positive impact, but it will also give your self-esteem a feel-good boost.
- **Finesse of forgiveness:** Set yourself free by learning to forgive yourself for past mistakes and failures. They weren't there to keep you hostage, rather they are there for you to learn and grow from.

- **Circumstance clarity:** Your circumstances do not define you. How you deal with them is what defines you. Keep your chin up, stick to your values, and trust that brighter days are on the horizon.

For an extra boost, ask yourself the following:

- What actions, habits, and thoughts can you adjust to balance your emotions and strengthen your resilience?
- What can you do to start cultivating a stronger relationship with yourself to foster a stronger sense of self-acceptance?
- How would your life change three months from now if you remained committed to achieving your goal?
- What's the biggest obstacle that stands between you and your happiness, and what actions can you take to overcome it?
- Name one small change you can bring about this week to make you feel more empowered.
- What are the things that motivate and excite you, and how can you incorporate them into your routine more consistently?
- What was one of the last things you did that made you feel confident?
- What can you do to contribute to healthier, more fulfilling relationships with your family and friends?
- How can you spend more time with people that support and nurture you?

Regret, Discomfort, and Personal Growth

Ah, the two things we fear most: regret and discomfort. But, why the bad rap? Because they're the ultimate reality check, forcing us to step outside of our cozy little bubbles and tweak our habits, thoughts, or behaviors.

Instead of thinking regret and discomfort are all doom and gloom, why don't you do a little perspective shift on the matter and see them as tools for personal growth instead? They are all instances that come about, like road signs, indicating where we need to pivot to refine ourselves. They're not punishments; they're messengers indicative of expansions and a deeper understanding of yourself and the world around you. Sure, uncertainty is uncomfortable and it's not easy to be vulnerable when you're forced to venture beyond the confines of your comfort zone. In truth, it requires effort, perseverance, resilience, and an open mind to step into the unknown. It's rather daunting but absolutely necessary! Nobody ever got anywhere exciting by staying in their pajamas all day, right?

It doesn't mean when things don't go your way, life's working against you. You see, life's always working for you and, sometimes, it provokes you to do a little introspection, demanding that you be intellectually agile. Think of going to the gym, for instance. Lifting the heavy stuff or stretching those legs isn't exactly as pleasing as lying on the couch and binge-watching a Netflix series. However, the discomfort makes you stronger in the long run. And, just as your muscles have to be subjected to some form of stress to strengthen and develop, the same goes for your mind and emotions. Every setback is like a little mental boot camp, toughening you up for whatever life throws your way.

The trick lies in how you perceive those moments and how you respond to them. Are they roadblocks or opportunities? You need to challenge the status quo, step into the unknown, and confront that discomfort to transcend your own limitations to unlock your full potential. Personal growth, in essence, is freedom. It liberates you from the self-imposed straightjacket of self-doubt, fear, and stagnation.

So, it's best to buckle up, buttercup, and embrace change and all that accompanies it to expand your awareness and reach a higher level of consciousness.

Stress Management Strategies

Change often comes with a side serving of stress. You didn't order it but got it anyway. It's pretty much part of the human experience.

There's no arguing that it can become all-consuming and extremely detrimental to your overall health, but thank your lucky stars that there are things you can do to better manage stress, keeping it at a minimum.

The following are some simple strategies that will help you combat stress and, in general, contribute to a more well-rounded existence:

- Keep a positive attitude by focusing on the silver lining in situations.
- You can't control everything, you have to accept that. Let go of what's out of your control and focus on what you can control.
- Be assertive and not aggressive. Be responsive and not reactive.
- Employ effective time management strategies and prioritize your to-do list to curb stress and anxiety.
- Use the word "no" more often. Start saying "yes" to your mental health and decline requests that spread you too thin.

- Be sure to make time to do the things that bring you true joy and fulfillment.
- Steer clear from any external stimulants, such as drugs and alcohol, in an attempt to soothe stress. It's just a recipe for an addictive disaster.
- Spend time with people who uplift and support you.
- Reach out to a mental health professional to learn about healthy ways to cope with stress.

Overcoming Self-Doubt and Anxiety

What if I don't make it? What will they think? What was I thinking?

Does any of this sound familiar? Of course, it does! It's yours truly: self-doubt. Yup, it's pretty standard, but only in small amounts. When you constantly walk around questioning your validity about everything it can be rather debilitating, preventing you from reaching your full potential.

Coupled with a whole host of unpleasantness such as fear and anxiety, self-doubt comes in three flavors:

- **Imposter syndrome:** You feel like a fraud.
- **Self-sabotage:** You undermine yourself and your goals.
- **Indecisiveness:** You're paralyzed by fear of making the wrong decisions.

These doubts slowly chip away and erode your self-esteem, leaving you with a negative view of pretty much everything, including yourself. Well, it stops here, today! Because you don't have to be stuck with this type of negativity forever.

The following tips will help silence that negative, nagging inner voice:

- Validation comes from within. Stop seeking external approval and rather focus on yourself, as well as your strengths, values, and achievements.
- Speaking of achievements, take a victory lap and celebrate yourself by listing all the things you've achieved in life.
- Stick to the positives and keep an eye on your self-talk. Remember, talk to yourself like you would to your best friend because you too are deserving of all the love and respect in this world.
- Pep talk yourself with positivity and churn out some affirmations or high-five yourself in the mirror to rev up your confidence motor.
- Appreciate and respect yourself. You're one of a kind, so be gentle.
- Stay in your lane and stop comparing yourself to others. Your journey is unique, with its own sets of challenges and victories.
- When in doubt, remind yourself of all the things that truly matter to you most. Stay true to yourself and stick to your values.
- Take regular social media detoxes to stay in touch with the real world.
- Keep yourself grounded by practicing awareness and engaging all your senses in the current moment.
- Do more of the things that make you feel good!
- Gratitude is the attitude that's always trending. Take time out every day to appreciate all the good stuff in your life.
- Remember, you're stronger than what you think.

We all have experienced an annoying person who shows up and overstays their welcome. Well, meet anxiety, fear's cousin who just creeps in when you least need or expect it.

Your heart starts racing, you gasp for air like an unfit marathon runner, and your palms become as sweaty as a pig at a bacon convention. Let's not forget the muscles feeling like they're going on strike! Then, to top it all off, your brain decides it's going to leave you feeling as sharp as a butter knife.

The problem with all of this? Anxiety can hang around for days on end, messing around with your eating habits, sleeping routines, and focus. Then, if anxiety turns the volume up a notch, we have panic attacks, which almost feel like you're having a heart attack of sorts. There are many different things that can elicit these responses and they all differ from person to person.

So, why do we feel like this when we're not actually in danger? It's ancient, we've been wired like this, and it's part of our survival instinct. The problem is that we don't have to worry about saber-tooth tiger attacks anymore but our brains still treat modern-day worries, like bills and social escapades, as if they're life-or-death situations. Yet again, anxiety, like stress, is manageable.

- **Own your emotions:** Don't try to ignore your experiences, it's not going to make your anxiety disappear. Instead, give it a name, visualize it as a shape or color, and doodle it out. It's like opening a window and letting out the stuffy air so you don't leave your emotions cooped up inside of you.
- **Do a body scan:** Check in with your body to detect where you're feeling tense. Start from the toes and work your way to the top of your head, or vice versa. If you detect some tension in a certain area, simply close your eyes, take

a couple of deep breaths, and visualize the tension melting away.

- **Challenge those thoughts:** Your thoughts love to play tricks, turning molehills into mountain peaks. Challenge those thoughts on a sheet of paper and get crafty—tear it up to represent your fears, then create a new contrasting piece that reflects your inner calm. Remind yourself that everything's going to be okay. Tomorrow's sunrise is another day in paradise.
- **Calm over chaos:** Steer clear of the chaos that sets off your anxiety. Take your energy and channel it into activities that will uplift, soothe, and inspire you. Create some art, read a book, or listen to some soothing music to help shift your focus and ease the discomfort.

Embrace Your Authentic Self

In a world where everyone seems to be striving to become the latest social media clone, being your authentic self and embracing your uniqueness is the ultimate power move! It's time to say "au revoir" to the cookie-cutter mindset and celebrate your one-of-a-kind awesomeness.

When we talk about being authentic, it refers to staying true to yourself in any given situation. And, what happens when you do this? You're not just being real, you become magnetic because people are drawn to authenticity, fostering deeper connections. It pretty much boils down to the concept of the value of rare things: the basic economic principle of supply and demand. When something is rare, there's less of it to go around. This creates a sense of exclusivity, making it more valuable and desirable, and enhancing its uniqueness.

Your uniqueness is your very own special blend of talents, perspectives, and quirks, all perfectly combined to make, well, you!

What about the haters? The only judgment that truly matters is your own because you're the only one who has the power to live your life to the fullest. Instead of trying to fit into societal ideals, become an inspiration and break free from the shackles of conformity. And, it all starts with knowing yourself—inside and out.

What are your values, passions, and dreams? What makes you tick? What puts an authentic smile on your face? Why opt for anything else if you can be part of the exceptional 1% of trailblazers who aren't afraid of coloring outside the lines? Greatness is within each and every one of us, just waiting to be embraced.

EMBRACING HEALTH AND WELLNESS

I get it, to-do lists can end up being longer than your arm. Welcome to the real world Also, there's one more very important thing to add: a regular health checkup. It's time to take charge of your health because it's an act of self-love.

Nothing is more important than your well-being, and that's why regular health checkups are extremely necessary, especially during times of change. The whole you will be checked up on—mentally, physically, and socially—to ensure everything is working in tip-top shape and you're on track with developmental milestones. These check-ups go beyond just taking your temperature, they're also a safe space for you to discuss those awkward body changes, stresses, anxieties, and even relationships. These visits also include important vaccinations to keep you protected. Nothing is taboo, and your doctor's only goal is to support your health, make you feel understood, and find solutions for any challenges early.

Make these regular checkups a priority, as they contribute to a more comfortable, confident you.

The Basics

The first and probably most important "health 101" fact: The habits you build now last for life. The earlier you start with a rocking self-care routine that nourishes mind, body, and soul, the better. And, it most certainly isn't rocket science. Here are a couple of tips that will be well worth sticking to for a healthier, brighter future:

Fuel your body properly

- Eat fruits, veggies, whole grains, and lean protein. Limit your intake of processed foods.
- Stay hydrated by drinking water instead of sodas.
- See food as medicine to make you feel good, otherwise, medicine is going to become your "food."

Never skimp on sleep

- Aim for 8-10 hours of sleep per night.
- Set a regular bedtime and stick to it.
- Unwind pre-sleep by reading or meditating vs scrolling.

Get moving

- Find physical activities you genuinely enjoy.
- The goal is at least 60 minutes of exercise daily. But, start slow, even if it's just an initial 10 minutes to get the ball rolling.
- Listen to your body and don't overdo it.

Feed your spirit

- Hang out with positive people who support and uplift you.
- Open up and talk about worries to a trusted friend, family member, or counselor.
- A friend in need is a friend indeed. Lean on loved ones when life gets tough. Asking for help is a strength, not a weakness.

Mental and Emotional Health

Your mental and emotional health plays a big role when it comes to your quality of life. So, it's best to start incorporating some awesome self-care rituals like meditation or journaling into your daily routine for a happy heart and a sunny mind.

Think of it as your judgment-free moments, where you get to assess and challenge those negative thoughts.

Let's jump right in, starting from the top!

Top 10 Tips for Improving Your Mental Health

1. Make self-care a regular habit! Set aside chill time to recharge—whether it's reading, journaling, or yoga, make self-care a regular habit!
2. Catch negative thoughts and swap them for kinder ones, talking to yourself with plenty of love and sincere compassion.
3. Tap into nature's healing benefits and spend time among trees or water to feel grounded and peaceful.
4. Venting helps! Lean on your loved ones when the going gets tough. Asking for support takes courage but pays off.

5. Boost your mood by focusing on blessings, so make gratitude a daily thing.
6. Prioritize sleep for an emotional lift, aiming for 8-10 hours a night.
7. Exercise regularly with movement that makes you sweat and smile.
8. Be present by noticing when your mind wanders, then gently bringing your focus back to the now. Meditation is your key when it comes to building that awareness muscle.
9. You are what you eat! Nourish yourself with whole, nutrient-dense foods and stay hydrated.
10. Laughter truly is great medicine. Seek out light-hearted moments daily, whether with friends or through comedy.

11 Powerful Mindfulness Practices

- **Deep breathing:** To calm your system, simply inhale, fill up your belly, and slowly exhale out your mouth.
- **Paced breathing:** The slow exhale works wonders to drop the heart rate. Inhale for 5 counts, exhale for 7.
- **Muscle relaxation:** Great for releasing stress throughout the body. Tense up then release muscle groups to unwind.
- **Meditation:** This is a very important exercise to help keep you grounded. Sit comfortably and focus on keeping a natural breath flow. Gently return attention to your breath when the mind wanders. Start with just 5 minutes.
- **5-4-3-2-1 grounding:** A quick and easy grounding exercise for those surprise anxious moments to bring you back to the present. Name 5 things you see, 4 you can feel, 3 you can hear, 2 you can smell, and 1 you can taste.
- **Body scans:** A fantastic pre-exam stress buster to release tension with breaths. Bring attention to each body part, noticing sensations. Release tension with breaths.

- **Journaling:** Free write your thoughts and feelings without editing or judging. Super cathartic!
- **Mindful movement:** This is a fun one to get in touch with yourself and tune into physical sensations during exercise. Put on some soothing music, or your favorite song, and completely submerge yourself in the moment, dancing and moving like nobody's watching. Walking works great too!

Practice Tips

- Find what you genuinely enjoy, and then it won't feel like work.
- Start small—brief moments add up.
- Pair with existing habits for consistency.
- Create little rewards as you meet mini-goals.
- Pick the right time of day based on your energy.
- Recruit a friend for accountability.
- Have a menu of options so you can switch it up.
- Use phone alerts to remind yourself.

ORGANIZATIONAL MASTERY

So, how do we own our days? We get organized, people! Yes, that might sound boring, but it makes all the "diffs" in the world. I'm talking less stress, less anxiety, and less freaking out about the tiniest things.

Planners, to-do lists, apps, there's so much you can do to prep and feel in control of your life. It's all about creating little appointments with yourself that will maximize your productivity!

- Stick to a routine to automatize good habits by creating daily to-do lists.

- Prep for the following day the night before, laying out your clothes and packing your bags.
- Create your own meal plan that will encourage healthier eating.
- Do those dishes daily to avoid the overwhelm caused by pile-ups.
- Declutter your wallet, file receipts, and chuck out irrelevant items.
- Always carry a notepad and a pen to jot down those "on-the-go" ideas.
- Stick to consistent spots for keys, chargers, and other daily items.

Tip-Top Document Tips

Documents are unavoidable companions in this wonderful world of ours. Whether it's electronic or paper, trust me, it's super important to keep these organized; it's your golden key to sanity. No need to hit a frantic paper shuffling panic in a desperate hunt for vital information, simply heed the following pearls of wisdom:

- Only keep what is necessary and relevant to avoid clutter.
- Categorize your documents by naming and dating files and folders to identify their contents.
- Archive any documents that you don't need and keep the current ones in an easily accessible spot.
- Make paper copies digital to eliminate storage constraints and improve sharing ability.
- Back up all your documents, making sure you have extra copies of all the important stuff.

Time Management

Life is truly a balancing act and effective time management is the skill you'll need to stay on the ball. Without it, you'll just end up buying an express ticket to "Freakout County." Creating a schedule and allocating your time effectively will make you more productive, enabling you to balance your commitments more efficiently, steer clear of procrastination station and distractions, and keep you motivated.

So, let's get organized:

- **Schedule and prioritize:** Prioritize your most important tasks and get them out of the way first when creating your schedule. This will curb anxiety and ensure you nail those deadlines.
- **Use tech:** Make technology work for you and hone some helpful time management apps. Set reminders and track your progress by making use of Google Calendar or Trello for instance.
- **Eliminate distractions:** Remove all distractions that will cause a wobble in your workflow, ensuring all your attention is focused on the task at hand and getting it done.
- **Multitask:** Now, I am not saying you have to turn into an octopus. Keep it real and effective with multitasking, like listening to lectures while you commute.
- **Productivity techniques:** There are ample productivity techniques such as the Pomodoro technique and Eisenhower Matrix, to name a few. Do a bit of research, exploring these techniques, and find one that will best facilitate our needs.

- **Take breaks:** As important as it is to get work done, it's just as important to take some time to rest and recharge. Be sure to schedule some rest periods into your schedule to avoid burnout.

HANDS-ON ELEMENT: CULTIVATE YOUR PERSONAL GROWTH PLAN

Oh yes, you do know all about self-worth, health and wellness, and organizational mastery! Gold stars all around! But, it's time to get practical about these aspects and whip them into healthy daily habits by creating a tailored plan for your very own needs and goals.

Let's get started!

1. **Self-evaluate:** Reflect on areas where you can improve your personal growth. Think self-confidence, organization, and stress management. What do you want to develop?
2. **Set those goals:** Set clear, realistic goals based on your evaluation. Keep it simple and be sure that they are SMART (specific, measurable, achievable, relevant, and time-bound).
3. **Action plan:** Create a step-by-step action plan for each goal. For instance, set time aside every Sunday to plan your week ahead. Make sure to include all the resources you might need, like meditation or time management apps and books.
4. **Implement:** Simply start taking action and keep it consistent.
5. **Track your progress:** Keep a journal or use an app to track your progress and review your goals.

Remember to stay flexible and keep an open mind. Self-improvement is not a quick fix; it's an ongoing journey. Seek support from loved ones who will help keep you accountable and stick to your goals. Always reflect and check in with yourself and your goals. How are things working out? What's working and what's not working for you? Pivot where required to lay the foundation for lifelong habits that will boost your well-being and contribute to your success.

Alright, my soon-to-be independent amigos, the clock's ticking down to your freedom to launch into the world of solo living! But, what are all the things you should know for independent living?

SKILL SHARING FOR A GENERATION

"No matter what age you are, growing up is scary."

THE GROWN-UP SCHOOL

I threw a ton of statistics at you in the introduction, so I wouldn't be surprised if one or two have slipped your mind at this point. Let me remind you of one significant one: of the 87% of parents who thought they were adequately preparing their kids to fly the nest, the majority of them doubted their teen's abilities to master the basics of adulting. Why is that?

Well, here's a secret: Not many adults are all that confident about adulting, either. That's in part because no one ever feels like they've quite got a handle on life. (Remind yourself of that one next time you feel overwhelmed!) And it's also because they weren't taught these lessons themselves. *They* didn't feel like they were ready to adult efficiently when they left home.

Life skills have long been overlooked when it comes to preparing kids to transition into adulthood, and your parents' generation missed out, too. This stuff has never been taught in school, and we're all at the mercy of our parents' knowledge. Often, what they teach us explicitly is much less than we need. So everyone's in the same boat, but your generation has a unique advantage: Books like this one are designed to show them the way.

Now that you're this far through, I'd like to ask you to take a moment and make the road a little easier for other teens like you. All you need to do to help them kickstart their discovery of the skills they'll need for a comfortable transition into adulthood is leave a short review.

By leaving a review of this book on Amazon, you'll show new readers exactly where they can find all the essential information they don't even know they need yet.

There's so much reward to be found in helping others, and by taking a few moments to do this, you'll know that you did something to help someone else out, and who better to do that than you —someone who's going through the exact same things that they are?

Thank you so much for your support. Now, let's get back to it!

Scan the QR code below

CHAPTER FIVE

ESSENTIAL DAILY LIVING SKILLS

Yup, it's all exciting until your bank account starts spilling the beans on the cost of living! Trust me, it hits like a ton of bricks. Suddenly, your weekly splurges and impulse buys aren't that glamorous anymore—and this is just the tip of the iceberg!

You see, Uber Eats is not going to cut it on a daily basis, you need to know how to cook, separate colors when it comes to doing laundry, understand oil changes, and a whole list of other things to best avoid total DIY disasters. There's a whole lot more to life than just having your own space and eating whatever you want.

Stepping into adulthood means more freedom, and with it, more responsibilities. But fear not, life skills are like practical magic, enabling you to hustle through the grind of daily life responsibly. The other great news? You'll be way more independent and self-sufficient!

Take notes; the real world waits for no one! Ready, set, learn!

NAVIGATING GROCERIES AND COOKING

Let's dish about nutrition so that you can crush it in the health department by making better chow choices. After all, if you want unstoppable energy you have to give your body the proper fuel.

Let's look at what a wholesome daily diet consists of:

- Kick your day off with a wholesome whole-grain cereal and fruit.
- Try to avoid sugar, refined carbs, and other processed foods as much as possible to curb those blood sugar crashes.
- Pack in at least five fiber-rich fruits and veggies to top up your vitamins, minerals, and antioxidants to stimulate growth and immunity.
- Enjoy some heart-healthy oily fish, such as sardines or salmon, at least twice a week.
- Keep an eye on those carbs, opting for whole grains over refined versions to help you feel fuller for longer.
- Limit saturated fats in meat and dairy products.
- Cut back on products with added sugars, which can negatively impact weight and dental health over time.
- Proceed with caution when it comes to your sodium intake.
- Drink enough water to stay hydrated.
- Lean into healthy proteins like chicken breasts, eggs, beans, peas, and tofu. The options are endless!

When in doubt, stick to fresh and unpackaged ingredients. You know, all the stuff your grandma will recognize! If it comes straight from the Earth, you're golden.

Let's break it down:

Instead of This:	Opt for This:
Refined breads and baked goods, like croissants or biscuits	Whole grain varieties, such as wheat or rye bread
Sugar-laden cereals and pastries	Steel-cut oats, low-fat granola, whole-grain cereals, or English muffins, which offer more nutrition
Buttery popcorn and salty, fried chips	Unsalted pretzels or plain popcorn
Bleached white refined flour	100% whole wheat flour
White pasta and white rice	Whole-wheat pasta and brown rice
Creamy, fatty sauces	Vegetable-based sauces

With a couple of minor, simple substitutions to your starches and grains, you can still enjoy all kinds of foods while boosting nutritional value.

Economical Grocery Shopping

When it comes to saving cash on groceries, it's a piece of cake! And, here are the perfect skills to hone the art:

- Get organized with meal planning to eliminate the "what's for dinner" headache in advance and only buy what you need.
- Utilize apps like SuperCook to find recipes based on ingredients you already have.
- Buy non-perishable items, like pasta, in bulk; less waste equals more savings!
- Frozen fruits and vegetables can be your cost-effective BFF.
- Temptation lurks at every turn, so stick to the plan and your grocery list to avoid impulse purchases, especially in the snack aisle.

- Skip shopping with a hungry belly at all costs!
- Finally, hit up digital coupons, loyalty programs, and rescuing expiring goods from apps like Flashfood.

Essential Cooking Skills

Let's step beyond microwaving and equip you with some essential kitchen skills and tips for a tasty victory!

- Become besties with boiling to whip up some tasty pasta and hearty soups. Boiling is more than just water making bubbles, there are different types of boils, such as:

  - Rolling at 212°F for eggs and pasta.
  - Slow at 205°F for broths and stock.
  - Simmer between 205 to 190°F for beans.

- Nail down basic knife skills to chop, slice, and dice ingredients with even flair for an even cook. Start by mastering the art of cutting an onion. Generally, start by trimming off the top, then halving lengthwise, and working your way from there.
- Learn to season and salt as you go to bring out some extra flavor.
- Experiment with making your own vinaigrettes to learn how to balance fats, acids, and emulsions for zesty dressings and spreads.
- Try your hand at roasting veggies to achieve that crispy, more flavorful goodness with high heat. Simple yet scrumptious!
- Explore searing to lock in delicious textures and juices when cooking your proteins like steak. It's all about

maintaining a perfect balance with a hot pan, minimal oil, and keeping your food dry.

- Deglaze (adding some liquid to a hot pan to lift off all the flavorful bits) pans to make lip-smacking flavourful sauces. You can add a good dash of herbs and butter for the finishing touch.
- Practice perfectly cracking eggs without getting shells in your meals. A simple, solid whack on the table is your way to go.
- Learn the art of whipping cream and egg whites to create delicious airy delights. This means you will have to understand the difference between soft, medium, and stiff peaks.
- Experiment with simmering beans or stocks for a creamy finish in your dishes.
- Always read the entire recipe, from start to finish, before you start working your magic to avoid any surprises along the way.
- Experiment with ingredient swaps and make notes while you cook to remember what worked and what didn't.
- Most importantly, always clean as you go.
- Regularly do taste tests to adjust seasoning when needed.
- If you don't have all the ingredients, look into alternatives. There are often plenty of more affordable and equally tasty options.
- Texture talks and matters as much as taste, so always keep an eye on the consistency of your dishes.
- You can do some improv while you're cooking; however, steer clear of any party tricks when it comes to baking. It's a precise process.
- Stick to what you know when it comes to cooking for guests and save the experiments for your own taste bud adventures.

VEHICLE KNOW-HOW

Itching to put the pedal to the metal for your very own first sweet ride? Well, buckle up buttercups, because there are a few things you need to know before buying your first car and cruising off into the sunset.

- Understand all the finances involved in buying a car. There are dealership fees, down payments, monthly interests, fuel expenses, tolls, insurance, repairs, and much more.
- Be sure to have an exemplary credit score because this will directly affect your eligibility for loans and those pesky interest rates.
- The bigger, the better when it comes to cash deposits! Aim to put down a solid 10 to 20% as a down payment.
- Avoid spending more than 10% of your monthly interest on transportation.
- Are you going to purchase or finance? Understand your options and implications of buying outright or financing your car purchase through a loan. Loans can help buy a car sooner, but be wary of those interest rates.
- What's your purpose for buying a car? Consider all specs and factors, such as passenger seating, fuel efficiency, safety features, and manufacturer recalls.
- Sure, used cars are a cheaper option, however, they may come with financing challenges, as well as potential safety and maintenance issues. Research and inspect used cars thoroughly before any purchase.
- Test drive the car before making any final decisions. A good tip: Ask a mechanic for a pre-purchase inspection to check for safety issues, previous accidents, and potential repairs.

- Do your homework and research the average selling price of the car to understand your negotiation leverage for a fair deal.
- Always read the fine print before signing anything!
- Car insurance is mandatory to cover accidents, third-party liability, and property damage. Research different insurance providers or ask a broker to help you choose the right coverage for your needs.

Basic Car Maintenance

It's all great to have your new wheels, but maintaining your car to be in tip-top condition is extremely important; your life and the lives of others are at stake every time you get behind that wheel.

I know it causes some auto anxiety when you look at it that way, but there's no turning a blind eye to this fact. So, let's get a better grasp on how you can play it safe and get some extra mileage out of your ride. Kicking off with the basics such as regular fluid checks and tire pressure may be stating the obvious, but staying on top of that stuff prevents major repair bills and keeps you safe! So, pop that hood and take a peek at the coolant, antifreeze, steering, and transmission fluid levels using dipsticks or gauges.

Regularly rotate your tires to help them wear evenly, and inspect tire pressure and tread depth. You can pop into a vehicle maintenance center, scheduling it on your maintenance to-do list along with your oil change trips (follow factory guidelines on mile/month swap-outs). While you're at it, keep an eye on those wiper blades and replace them if they're ragged, making stripy wipes.

Listen for any new squeaks, rattles, or rumbles, and take immediate action. Ignoring sounds or smells can snowball, eventually causing bigger headaches. Nobody wants to be stranded and, trust me, this usually happens when least expected!

Now that we have the bare basics out of the way, here are some other important factors to keep tabs on:

- Check your battery and look for any damage, such as cracks, frayed cables, and corrosion.
- Inspect your air and cabin filters and replace them if needed.
- Check out your vehicle manual or Google factory guidelines for spark plug replacement intervals. Generally, when your car has difficulty accelerating or misfires, it's due to some spark plug damage.
- Then, there are the belts like the serpentine and timing belts. If these babies are cracked, frayed, or loose, it's time for a replacement.
- Regularly check your lights, such as headlights, tail lights, and indicators, to make sure they shine brightly and work properly. This will include your engine light.

There's quite a bit to cover; thus if you're not sure, your best bet is to reach out to a professional—whether it be a mechanic or the dealership. Never slack on your maintenance schedule, it will only shorten your ride's lifespan!

Driving Tips

That new license means freedom's calling from the open road! So, let's ensure you heed the need for safety.

- **Stick to traffic rules!** There are no loopholes here. Thus, be sure to familiarize yourself with all the road signs and traffic signals.

- **Always remain within the prescribed speed limits.** They are there for a reason—to ensure safety.
- **Slow down, you're not in a race.** When hit a higher speed, you are essentially reducing your reaction time, which worsens the impact of collisions.
- **Just as your body needs regular checkups to operate optimally, so does your car.** So, schedule your regular maintenance checkups to ensure longevity and reliability.
- **Buckle up!** Wear your seat belt and ensure your passengers do the same to lower the risk of injuries and fatalities in accidents.
- **When you're driving, well, you're driving.** No eating, making reels, or searching around in your glove compartment. Eyes on the prize: the road.
- **Check your mirrors.** Adjust your seat and mirrors for comfort and visibility, ensuring blind spots are covered.
- **Never tailgate.** Follow the 3-second rule to maintain a safe distance from vehicles ahead.
- **Have all important documents within reach.** Keep all the necessary documents, such as proof of insurance, vehicle registration, and license, in your car.
- **Be prepared.** Make sure your emergency kit is properly stocked at all times.
- **Keep your eye on the weather forecast to gauge driving behavior.** In wet weather, drive with your headlights on, increase your following distance, and drive slower.
- **Absolutely refrain from driving under the influence of alcohol or other substances, including when you're tired.** Instead, hop onto some public transport to keep yourself and others safe.

Fixing a Flat

Just like bad hair days, flat tires happen. Not to worry, because there's always a quick fix you can do to get things all smoothed out.

First things first: Understand the difference between permanent and temporary tire repairs. The emergency roadside plug and repairs are temporary and meant to get you to a service center for a proper repair. But, understanding how to do a temporary roadside repair is important.

Here is the nifty R.E.P.A.I.R. process:

- **Remove:** You have to remove the tire off the wheel for a proper inspection.
- **Evaluate:** Upon spotting the puncture, assess the angle and size, and inspect for any cord and belt damage.
- **Prepare:** Clean and buff the damaged area, ensuring maximum adhesion.
- **Apply:** Next, apply the vulcanizing fluid and give it enough time to dry properly.
- **Install:** Insert the repair plug through the hole in the tire and attach it to the inside of the tire to get rid of any trapped air.
- **Return to service:** Remount the tire and inflate it. Make your first stop at a service center for a proper permanent repair.

BEING EMERGENCY READY

Sure, prepping an emergency kit might be as much fun as watching paint dry, but there's no negotiating when it comes to safety!

Taking a couple of precautions before the unexpected strikes can save your hide big time. A well-stocked emergency kit gives you peace of mind that can help transform panic into plan. Let's take a look at the basics when it comes to your car and home emergency safety kits:

Emergency Car Kit

- Your standard first-aid kit. Keep it in the glove compartment or the trunk.
- A blanket, flashlight (with spare batteries), gloves, tarp, and a raincoat.
- A car charger. An inexpensive mobile phone is also highly recommended.
- Bottled water and snacks for both pets and passengers.
- Cleaning supplies, like paper towels, wet wipes, or rags, including a snow brush and ice scraper.
- Emergency car warning devices, such as reflectors and flares.
- A basic tool kit, along with duct tape.
- Jumper cables and a portable jump pack.
- Traction aids, such as salt or sand.

Emergency Home Kit

- tweezers
- scissors
- digital thermometer
- safety pins
- disposable gloves
- adhesive tape
- different sized plasters
- triangular bandages

- gauze dressings in different sizes
- alcohol-free cleansing wipes
- rolled crepe bandages
- two or more sterile eye pads
- eye wash solution
- distilled water
- antiseptic cream
- skin rash cream
- topical spray or cream for insect stings and bites
- antihistamine tablets or cream
- pain relief tablets, like paracetamol, ibuprofen, and aspirin

Common Emergencies

Life is unpredictable and, sometimes, the things we experience may not be pleasant, like common emergencies. It's important to understand the basics when life pulls a sneaky ambush to avoid panic attacks and bumbling around with bandaids on our heads, wondering what in the heck just happened!

Let's scan through some common emergencies and discuss how to address them effectively.

Bleeding

Wounds and cuts may lead to bleeding externally and internally. In general, bleeding can be easily managed at home, but seek immediate medical attention if:

- The bleeding doesn't stop.
- The wound appears to be deep.
- The wound has a foreign object embedded.
- If bone or tissue is visible.

- If significant blood loss signs appear like paleness, loss of consciousness, or dizziness.

Breathing Difficulties

Breathing difficulties are generally caused by allergic reactions, respiratory infections, asthma attacks, or choking. Some symptoms may include shortness of breath, chest tightness, wheezing, or rapid breathing. This is not something you want to play around with. Thus, the best thing to do is to remain calm and immediately contact medical emergency services.

Collapse

Collapsing or fainting affects breathing and consciousness. If someone faints and is not breathing, immediately call medical emergency services. If they are still breathing, gently put them in the recovery position and seek help.

- **The recovery position:** Place the person on their side with their upper leg bent and their head tilted back to keep the airway clear.

Seizures

Seizures can be recognized by involuntary shaking or minimal movement and altered consciousness. Never restrain a person who's experiencing a seizure. Protect them from injury by removing any potentially harmful objects. Seek medical attention after the seizure, especially if it lasts longer than five minutes.

Pain

Pain comes in all forms and is generally brought on by injury or illness. Pain relief medication does come in handy, depending on the severity. If the pain persists and is unbearable though, it's best to seek medical attention.

Heart Attacks

Heart attacks always require emergency medical attention! They occur when there's a sudden blockage of blood flow to the heart and include symptoms such as chest pain, pain in the left arm, nausea, sweating, dizziness, and shortness of breath.

Stroke

A stroke occurs when blood flow to the brain is disrupted due to a blood clot or brain bleed. This can be recognized by a drooping face, weakened arms, and speech difficulty. Seek immediate medical attention! It's important to minimize long-term damage caused.

Planning for the Unexpected

What will you do if you're caught in a superstorm? No lights, no wi-fi, no going outside? Are you prepared for the unexpected?

This is a serious question. Think about it and consider the possibility of a common disaster in your area. What do you think you'll need to survive during that time? Medications, communication, food, and money?

Well, there are three steps you need to prepare for the unexpected: a plan, a kit, and staying informed.

Let's look at the main aspects you have to consider:

- **Health:** Be sure you have your medications stocked, and some extra put aside. There's no running a quick errand to the pharmacy during a disaster.

- **Finances:** How will you pay for things? Be sure to have some cash on hand. If systems are down and you don't have access to the internet, cash is king.
- **Friends and fam:** Consider having an emergency phone and some power banks on hand. Regularly check and ensure that your power banks are charged. Make a spare set of keys and give them to your family or trusted friends. This way, if you're injured and they need access to you, they'll have a way to reach you.
- **Mind:** Pack some board games and a couple of good reads to keep you entertained and curb boredom.
- **Documents:** Keep copies of all important documents, such as medical information, identification, and family contact information, in a fireproof safe or other protected space.
- **Evacuation plan:** Come up with an effective evacuation plan that you regularly practice and refine by asking the following questions:

  - How will you find your friends and family?
  - Where will you meet them or where will you go?
  - What routes can you take?
  - How will you get there?
  - How will you ensure a power source?

- **Prep kit:** A basic prep kit should consist of:

  - nonperishable food items
  - water
  - a first-aid kit
  - flashlight and spare batteries
  - emergency radio and spare batteries
  - a sufficient supply of medications
  - personal hygiene items and sanitizers

- ○ cash
- ○ area maps

HANDS-ON ELEMENT: DEVELOPING YOUR DAILY LIVING SKILLS

What a great set of skills we've just explored! And, yes, you've guessed it: It's time to put those skills into action. Here's a solid approach that will help you upgrade and streamline these skills from "eh" to "oh":

1. Grocery Shopping

A. Plan your grocery shopping by creating a shopping list that aligns with your meal plans and budget.

B. Compare prices, read the labels, and stick to healthy, budget-friendly options.

C. Steer clear from those impulse purchases and avoid hitting the store on an empty belly.

2. Cooking Skills

A. Don't be afraid to experiment with different recipes and ingredients.

B. Set a schedule at least once a week to explore some uncharted culinary territories.

C. Always write down what you test and try to document your winning combos.

3. Vehicle Maintenance

A. If you've got wheels, take some time and familiarize yourself with the maintenance manual.

B. Practice some basics like checking the tire pressure, oil, and windshield wipers. Feeling adventurous? Give jump-starting a go!

C. Hit up a mechanic or a seasoned car enthusiast for some pro tips.

4. Emergency Prep

A. Put together your first aid kits for both car and home. And, most importantly, don't overlook that emergency prep kit filled with items like first aid supplies, non-perishable food, water, and basic tools.

5. Personal Maintenance Schedule

A. Create a personalized maintenance schedule that covers your grocery shopping, meal preps, and vehicle checks. You can always adjust it based on your experience and lifestyle.

6. Improvement

A. Ask friends and family for feedback and any additional tips that may help you improve the skills you've been working on.

These skills might come across as basic, but their power reaches far beyond! Not only will they bolster your practical daily routine, but they will also significantly contribute to your independence and confidence. But, remember, it takes consistent practice!

Up next, it's all about the transformative power of travel. Yup, it's not just about where you go; it's also about immersing yourself in new experiences.

Let's learn!

CHAPTER SIX

TRAVEL WISDOM

We've all dreamt of just booking a flight and "peacing" out to somewhere awesome. Ah, just the thought of trying new foods, meeting cool people, and giving your routine a drop-kick for a while sounds so amazing! It's such an insatiable urge, isn't it?

Yeah, we've all heard that little voice in the back of our noggins, whisper, "What if…" and "Just imagine…" Just the thought is enough to make your heart skip a beat. No more clocks or studying, who wouldn't buy into that?

Of course, you can make it happen—and you should! Traveling isn't just a dream reserved for the wealthy. It opens up so many possibilities and you can learn so much from these experiences. But, with the budgeting, packing, transportation, safely navigating new environments, blah blah blah, it can get really overwhelming. Hey, the tools are there to map these things out!

So, grab your passport and get ready to make memories. What are you waiting for? The world's there for the taking and making of some incredible memories!

TRAVEL PLANNING AND BUDGETING

So, you "wanderluster," let's turn those travel dreams into reality and look at creating an effective travel budget. This is a very important first step that will help you establish realistic savings goals and make some better spending choices.

- **Transport:** How are you going to get there? Trains, planes, and automobiles! Look into different travel options and their associated costs. Never book any tickets before comparing prices, perhaps you might find a good deal somewhere.
- **Accommodation:** Where are you going to stay? Airbnb, hotel, motel, or hostel? Hostels and shared rooms can save you a significant amount of pennies. Keep an eye out for whether your crash pad offers at least one free meal a day.
- **Commuting:** How are you going to get from "A" to "B" when you're there? Calculate your average daily commute costs. There are great sites like Numbeo that provide some spot-on cost-of-living insights.
- **Food:** What will you do for grub? Hit up Numbeo to get an estimation of food prices. But, make sure to dine in and whip up your own grub at least once a day to save some cash.
- **Leisure and pleasure:** What are you going to explore? Make a wish list of all the attractions and activities with entry fees you want to check out. Sometimes, booking in advance comes with a significant discount!
- **Souvenirs:** What are you bringing home? You can't just travel and not return with a memento and a couple of gifts.

Set aside a shopping budget to pick up a couple of keepsakes.

- **Emergencies:** Always have spare cash set aside as an emergency fund for unexpected events, just in case.

Travel Deals and Saving Tips

There's nothing like scoring a sweet deal when it comes to travel—or pretty much anything in life for that matter. And, it's a fairly simple art to master!

First, make tech work for you and download some nifty apps like Scott's Cheap Flights and Hopper to help snag alerts on budget flights and hotels. Skyscanner is another good bet that publishes daily deals and steals. Twitter also has a couple of solid accounts you can follow for info, such as @JetBlueCheeps and @TPG_Alerts. There are plenty of similar accounts, just get out there and join a couple. They will keep you updated on the latest and greatest like mistake fares and last-minute flight deals.

Before you click and lock any deals, do some research to make sure that you're not dealing with sketchy airlines or accommodation scams. Also, look at layovers, takeoff times, and baggage fees. Compare the offers to regular costs because all that glitters isn't always gold. Also, make use of your points programs and miles, they stack up over time!

Hunting for some epic deals takes time, so be patient and keep your ears to the ground. Just a heads up though, these sell out fast so you have to pounce quickly!

PASSPORT AND GLOBAL EXPLORATION

A passport is your ticket to the world! Simply put, it's an official government ID that lets you cross borders and travel between countries. You 100% need this, baby!

Inside these booklets, you'll see your name, photo, date of birth, and citizenship status. The cool thing is that it also serves as your ID if you lose your wallet or license. If you ever get accused of overstaying your welcome overseas, that passport is what will save your tush, verify your identity, and prove you have a legal right to be there. It's your safeguard when you're far away from home.

An expired passport is as good as no passport, so be sure that you either have one or that yours is current and updated. How do you get or update this global access pass of yours?

Here's a rundown:

- Get your hands on a passport application and fill it out.
- Passports aren't free, so you'll have to cough up a fee for your application. But, hey, it's an adventure investment.
- Next, it's time to shine and get your passport photo taken. Remember, this is going into your passport, so make sure it's good.
- Just to make sure that you're really who you say you are, you will have to present some other forms of identification.
- When everything is filled out and signed, with all the added extras—like your pics and ID copies—it's time for the drop-off to an approved passport facility.
- Generally, it takes between 4 to 6 weeks to get your passport, but ensure that all your paperwork is in order to avoid any delays.

The Significance of a Passport for International Travel

Without your passport, you can pretty much kiss any international vacay goodbye. Not exactly music to a travel-hungry person's ears, right?

Let's dig a little deeper into why passports matter big time when it comes to living your best life and seeing the world.

Your passport is your ID, a little booklet complete with your name, rad photo, date and place of birth, citizenship status, and miscellaneous deets. This is what verifies to customs officials that you are who you say you are, enabling you to legally cross borders.

That little stamp of approval grants you instant access to endless adventure and life-changing experiences. But, here's the thing: Most countries require your passport to be valid for at least 6 months post-visit! So, before you book to jet off, keep an eye on that expiration date because an expired or soon-to-be expired passport means the only experience you'll have is heartache and crocodile tears, getting denied entry at your dream destination you planned and saved for. So, it's best to avoid that last-minute panic.

Then, there are the visas, which are just as important. These documents are directly linked to your passport number. However, without your passport, your visa is useless and you will still be refused entry. Both docs are 100% non-negotiable. And, depending on where you plan to travel, some visas need to be applied for and approved way before time. There are other forms of visas, like health travel documents, flight details, and accommodation reservations. It's always a good idea to double-check the country entry requirements closer to your departure because you never know what changes in this dynamic travel landscape.

So, unless you fancy getting dragged off flights, denied entry, or stuck indefinitely in foreign airports, be sure that you check all these boxes.

Responsible Tourism Practices

Ah, the calls to experience new flavors, traditions, landscapes, and ways of life! But, it's not all open hunting season when it comes to stepping foot onto a foreign land; you have to be a mindful, respectful explorer.

After all, who likes those arrogant, ignorant tourists who disrespect sacred sites and country customs? So, let's chat about responsibly embracing cultural sensitivity when traveling to avoid any cringe-worthy moments and truly connect with the richness that surrounds you.

- Research cultural customs and norms before jetting off by diving into blogs, travel sites, and guidebooks to get the lowdown. Understand the taboos, dress codes, and greetings to have respectful interactions.
- Put in a little effort and memorize a few polite phrases in the local language to impress.
- Once your toes hit the ground, immerse yourself! Observe how the locals go about their daily lives. Look at how they interact, transact, and act in public. Then, monkey see, monkey do; adopt similar body language and clothing styles to blend in better.
- If something is a bit of a head-scratcher, ask respectful questions for a clearer understanding. And, don't judge!
- Always respect cherished traditions and follow the appropriate guidelines when visiting historic or spiritual sites.

- Approach ceremonies and celebrations with an open mind and avoid gawking, each custom has a sacred meaning.
- Support the communities you're discovering by shopping local and supporting small businesses. Stay in locally-owned hotels and enjoy cultural experiences provided by area artisans and guides. This is not only empowering for locals but also helps preserve cultural customs.
- Not everything you see in the movies is real, so avoid stereotyping people and places. It's the array of perspectives that makes humanity beautiful. Differences are there to celebrate and learn from, not fear and judge.

Be conscious, and be mindful, this home we share is miraculously diverse!

INSURANCE AND SAFETY ESSENTIALS

Travel does come with risks, but what doesn't in this world? No need to be deterred, only be educated. So, it's best to get cozy with travel insurance and a couple of other facts.

Travel insurance means you've got backup when the unexpected comes knocking. And, the biggest reason for this would be medical emergencies. Getting injured or falling ill in a foreign country is no joke. Aside from that, the medical bills can really be a shocker most of the time!

However, good insurance will foot the bill so you don't go broke. It'll also cover if your bags get swiped, legal trouble looms, and flight cancellations pop up. Worst case scenario? If you pass away, it will cover transporting your remains back home. Morbid but essential.

As with everything, before you swipe and sign, read the fine print! The devil's in the details! These plans are all different, and some may have guidelines regarding pre-existing health conditions, certain activities, high-risk destinations, and a whole list of other factors to consider. Ask tons of questions!

Then, there are the basic safety precautions. Research your destinations thoroughly and be sure to register with your embassy. Keep your valuables and important documentation safe in a secure place, avoiding hob-knobbing around town and being all flashy. Avoiding sketchy situations goes without saying. Yes, it's great to meet new peeps, but be careful not to divulge sensitive information. There are some freaky people out there and, for many of them, their career is making a profit off of gullible tourists. Check in with a loved one on a daily basis and share your itinerary with them to ensure someone always knows where you are.

Last and most certainly not least, keep an eye on your bags and luggage when traveling between destinations to avoid any tampering, pickpocketing, or theft.

The bottom line: Travel insurance gives you peace of mind for happy, safe traveling.

Different Kinds of Travel Insurance

Whether you're backpacking, road-tripping, or catching waves anywhere in this wonderful world of ours, insurance needs to form part of your travel package. You might feel invincible now, but, trust me, you will regret skipping coverage if an emergency were to happen.

Let's unpack the lowdown on key types of insurance:

- **Medical insurance:** Hospital bills can rack up faster than a kid collecting Pokémon cards! Some places can even rack up five or six-figure bills! Medical coverage has you covered so you don't end up having heart failure on top of all things. It may also cover ER and doctor visits, prescriptions, and emergency flights back home. Other perks can also include 24/7 access to assistance centers, referrals for English-speaking doctors, and guarantees to pay hospitals upfront if they require it.
- **Trip cancellations:** If anything unexpected happens, such as a broken leg, before the day you head toward your destination, your insurance reimburses any prepaid costs such as flights and hotels. Some policies can even cover up to 100%! It's a good peace of mind for the unforeseeable.
- **Baggage insurance:** This insurance covers your luggage against loss, damage, and theft. This comes in handy when you're hopping around with pricey gadgets and keepsakes. Generally, airlines already cover checked bags if they are lost or get damaged as well.
- **Evacuation insurance:** This insurance will get you to the nearest hospital or treatment facility in an air ambulance or chartered plane during emergencies. This is a great safety net for those off-the-grid, remote adventures.
- **Other options:** There are other options, such as light insurance if a crash occurs, cancel for any reason policies, and vehicle collision coverage for rental cars.

The best thing you can do is chat with an agent and see what insurance best suits your needs. Get into the nitty-gritty details such as reimbursement limits, exclusions for pre-existing conditions, claim processes, covered reasons to cancel trips, and documents required.

Choosing the Right Insurance

Alright, having travel insurance is important, but how do you figure out which is best for you? There's actually a bit to consider, so let's figure it out.

- **Identify common claims:** What are the most common claims traveling folks make? Did you know that more than half of claims are for trip cancellations? It makes perfect sense; think family emergencies and weather issues, for instance. Yup, all the things that are outside of your control that can ruin your plans. Another huge chunk of claims is due to medical emergencies such as injuries, illness, and evacuations during travel.
- **Choose your coverage:** Right off the bat, you can see that your coverage should, at least, include both trip cancellation and medical coverage to safeguard your hard-earned funds. Knowing you're refunded during delays, cancellations, and health scares is a significant stress off the shoulders.
- **What are your options?** There are tons of options out there! Consider the nature of your adventure to tailor your coverage to your needs. Are you backpacking? Visiting ancient ruins? Which country are you going to?
- **Medicals:** Make sure that your medical coverage includes evacuation to good hospitals in dire situations. If you're an adrenaline junkie and into adventurous activities, be sure that your plan covers these extremes because "vanilla" plans generally exclude these things.

- **Existing coverage:** Review what existing coverage you might have to avoid duplicating coverage. Only cover the noticeable gaps to ensure your protection.
- **Fine print:** Compare your options for the best deals. Before signing anything, read that fine print! Be clear about what's covered, the claims process, the assistance and benefits provided, and how pre-existing health conditions factor in.
- **Extra tips:** Make sure your dream destination is covered by your policy. And, if traveling to remote places, confirm evacuation/transport is covered if needed. Oh, and avoid those budget plans unless you're overflowing with cash in your bank account to foot some hefty unexpected costs. For reassurance, connect directly with travel agents, and share your destination wishlist, archived medical concerns, and desired activities. Share anything relevant to make sure they suggest plans that legit have you fully covered!

HANDS-ON ELEMENT: CRAFTING YOUR PERSONAL TRAVEL PLAN

Are you ready to get out there, book a flight, and see the world? Of course, you are! So, let's kick off your epic quest and craft your own travel plan.

1. Destination Pick

A. Up first, pick a destination that gets you all excited and fired up. Is it a city? Perhaps an island?

B. Make Google your best friend and start researching all the ins and outs of your chosen spot. Check out attractions,

local customs, and safety tips to be in the know before
you go.

2. Budget

A. It's time to get real and look at all the money stuff. Create
a budget that covers all your expenses, from flights to daily
living expenses. Don't forget about those emergency funds!

B. Keep an eye out for deals and steals, like off-season
discounts, budget-friendly accommodations, and any travel
hacks to stretch your budget.

3. Travel Itinerary

A. Nothing like a good plan they say! Map out your time
with must-see spots and activities, spontaneous adventures,
and some chill time.

B. And, there's no good plan without a plan B. Be ready to
pivot because plans may change for various reasons, such as
bad weather and unexpected closures.

4. Travel Docs

A. Double-check all your travel documents and location
requirements. Make sure that your passport and visa are up
to date.

B. Make copies, both physical and digital, of all important
documents and keep them safe and secure.

5. Pack and Prep

A. Create a checklist based on your destination and trip duration. Remember to keep luggage limits in mind, so pack smart.

B. Leave some extra packing space for those souvenirs and gifts!

6. Health and Safety

A. Safety always comes first! Research any health precautions that are required for your destinations. Some places require medications or vaccinations.

B. Have all necessary emergency contacts saved and handy, just in case.

7. Cultural Sensitivity

A. Learn about the traditions and customs of your destination to avoid troublesome and awkward moments.

B. Learn some basic phrases, such as greetings and negotiation basics. Some good ones are "please," "thank you," and "help."

8. Post-Trip

A. After your trip, always take some time to reflect on your experience. What did you enjoy? What should you steer clear of?

B. Take notes for better future planning.

You're now ready to get out there and conquer the world! But, remember, it's not just about the destination, it's about the journey too! Make as many memories as you can so that they will last a lifetime. Savor each moment, laugh until your cheeks hurt, and appreciate the small things, no matter how oddly foreign they may seem. Because, one day, when you look back on this fun, crazy ride called life, you'll have memories that will stick with you forever, reminding you of how far you've come.

Now that you have the lowdown on the world, what about the digital world we find ourselves in? I am positive that you're already a pro when it comes to scrolling and navigating our World Wide Web. After all, tech has totally transformed the way we live, work, and play. We're uber-connected! But, are you informed about all the ways you can use the tools out there, not only for personal reasons but also for professional growth?

The digital world is more than just a place to kill time, you know?

CHAPTER SEVEN

DIGITAL LITERACY AND SAFETY

When was the last time you weren't glued to a screen? Phones, tablets, laptops, smartwatches, and desktops are everywhere!

Yup, all the gadgets and apps are pretty cool, but let's be real: It's a jungle out there. We have hackers, scams, privacy dramas, questionable content, and all sorts of freaky things. How does one thrive and stay secure in this realm? Well, don't worry. There are ample things you can do to become an epic "digizen" and harness the power of the web for good, stand out in smart ways, and guard your back against cyber creeps.

You'll need to know how to spot the fakes, research like a pro, keep your private info airtight, and hustle to snag opportunities. And, it's all completely possible to do without compromising your safety!

Let's take a look at how you can create killer content and make the web work for you—on your terms.

NAVIGATING THE DIGITAL WORLD

Oh, yes, between all the Instagram scrolling, TikTok dances, YouTube blackholes, and group chats blowing up our phones, the online world is pretty much our world 24/7.

The mighty internet is more than just our favorite apps and endless memes. It's legit been life-changing in regard to leveling up society. Beyond all the emojis and trends, it has completely revolutionized how we explore, learn, work, and access opportunities. Take education, for instance; there's no more endless paper and encyclopedias. Now, you're just a few clicks away from instantly accessing updated facts and research on, literally, any topic that comes to mind.

You can build your projects from your couch and access info in real time. Thanks to the internet, you can now become an overnight expert in Ancient Egyptian mythology, score some great grades through Khan Academy, or master software development through YouTube. Irrespective of your interests or goals, you have a wealth of information at your disposal to continually educate yourself, discover new things, and unleash your creativity.

Job searches are also not as agonizing compared to back in the day. No more rifling through newspapers or licking stamps to mail applications. You can easily browse job opportunities, submit applications online, get instant resume feedback, connect with bosses on LinkedIn, and even work remotely!

What about keeping up with friends and family across cities and continents? No more snail mail or scary phone bills, just a simple DM or video chat complete with memes and all. No one is truly disconnected anymore. Plus, coordinating hookups and gatherings has become as easy as pie. Do you remember the pandemic? How would we have sailed through that disaster without virtual classes, TikTok dances, and Netflix binges to maintain our sanity? E-hugs internet.

Political activism has also been amplified, and marginalized voices can now unite across the globe as one force! No more suppressed movements struggling to have their voices heard and get the facts out. This all happens at lightning speed in our modern "viral times." Nothing is off the table, including petition signatures and coordinated protests for collective action.

Then, there's our beloved Google Maps, which gets us, well, pretty much navigating anywhere without having to unfold a map the size of a fitted sheet. Never mind folding it back! Dating has become a whole different ball game when it comes to summoning a cute date with a simple swipe. Speaking about socials, can't make it to a concert? Simply hop online and you can access it virtually.

Healthcare and shopping have become quite an experience, with limitless reach and same-day service it saved more than a stitch in time! What about AI? Oh, and it just got started, making creative writing and content creation a breeze.

The options are truly limitless and what we have achieved so far is pretty awe-inspiring. The internet is a great tool that unites humanity and, if used for noble causes, it's life-changing!

Navigating Platforms Effectively

Using social media is boatloads of fun! But, tread with caution. Sure, it's easy to click and post, but, remember, you're essentially establishing your personal brand out there. Yes, you're painting a picture of your morals and values. Aside from this, effective social media use also protects you, preventing you from falling into traps like FOMO, toxic comparisons, loss of privacy, and even harassment.

Let's take a look at a couple of tips that will help you stay within your lane and navigate these platforms responsibly:

- **Always speak your truth to your folks and make them aware of the apps you use.** Sure, it may be a bit awkward, but they can give you some perspective and protection. They will never want to see you get hurt or feel pressured because of regrettable posts and interactions.
- **Think before you post, share, and comment.** There's always a consequence attached to an action. On the streets of Insta and TikTok, even "private" posts can easily get leaked and screenshotted. Remember, you can't erase the internet's memory!
- **Some things are best left to the imagination.** Don't overshare personal and private info and disable your GPS coordinates when sharing your location. Protect your space, you never know who's lurking.
- **Regularly review your privacy settings on platforms to dictate who has access to your content.** There's no need to mass broadcast every detail of your life.
- **Screen all your follow requests.** There are so many fake profiles, catfishes, and predators who have no issue exploiting others and stealing personal data. If you don't know them, don't accept them. Safety first!
- **Be kind and considerate when it comes to online engagement.** Things can easily be misunderstood without facial cues. Provide constructive feedback and thoroughly explain the context of your messages and posts to avoid any misunderstanding.

- **Prioritize your mental health and know when to log off.** If anything makes you feel inadequate or pressured, leave. Your self-worth is way more important. Prioritize real-life connections and set time limits on your platform usage.

Balancing Digital Life with the Real-World

Booting up your social media or Fortnite might feel more natural than breathing in this modern age. But, all that scrolling and gaming can make us easily forget that we're made up of flesh and blood, not binary codes.

We need to spend time offline and in the real world, enjoying the outdoors, face-to-face interactions, and a whole lot of other things. Spending time with real people develops empathy in ways that DMs and texts will never be able to. And, it's not just empathy; it's about balance in life. This is not a "devices are the devil!" take on things.

All these platforms have priceless perks, but too much of anything in this world is bad. You need to establish a solid soul foundation with yourself, others, and the world around you. Trust me, you'll laugh harder, talk more, and establish deeper bonds. External validation will not be as urgent, and your core emotional needs will be more fulfilled.

Let's look at some strategies to help you maintain a healthy balance between the digital and real world:

- **Firstly, you need to understand your habits.** Where do most of your online hours disappear? TikTok marathons? Snapchat streaks? Only when you can identify your habits can you make the necessary changes.

- **Little tweaks add up.** So, schedule some offline times when you can engage in activities without a screen. Read a book, go for a walk, people watch, or build a puzzle. Not everything vintage is cringe. Reflect on where you can bring about other changes, such as refraining from picking up your phone first thing in the morning or logging off one hour before bedtime.
- **Go out with your friends and do the unthinkable; leave your phone at home!** This might sound like pure insanity, but boredom sparks creative convos. If this all sounds too overwhelming, simply turn off app notifications when you hang with friends to avoid getting distracted.
- **Enrichment trumps entertainment!** Pick up a new hobby to increase engagement in more meaningful pastimes. Practice the guitar, learn a new language, join a yoga group, or cook a new cuisine! This will flip the script and substitute mindlessly moving from app to app.
- **If you find yourself struggling to disconnect, reflect on the possible reasons.** What's this void you're trying to fill? No judgment allowed, you don't need the added pressure. Perhaps you endlessly scroll because you're bored, lonely, or find reality too stressful. If you can pinpoint the underlying cause, you're halfway there.
- **Find other ways to express yourself.** Vent your anxieties through art or do a bit of journaling instead of complaining on Twitter. Make an effort to step away from all that external noise because the healthiest connection you can have is with yourself.

ONLINE SAFETY AND PRIVACY

Let's turn you into a super cyber security guru! Why? Because it's important to lock down your online safety!

Our digital playground is lit with opportunities, emojis, and funny memes. But, unfortunately, creeps and hackers are just as rife, hoping to jack your passwords, data, and peace of mind.

So, let's look at being smart and the know-how to protect yourself out there:

- **Oversharing isn't caring:** Remember how we talked about your "online reputation" becoming your brand? Well, future bosses and colleges stalk profiles to judge reputations and character. This all happens based on what you post. Nothing online, with or without privacy settings, ever fully disappears. So, think twice before you click "post."
- **Private details:** Avoid oversharing private info, like your phone number, addresses, and real-time locations. Turn off your GPS coordinates, and location tracking is an absolute no-go.
- **Block and report:** Block and report any sketchy posts, people, and fake stuff to prevent scams and abuse, protecting yourself and the online community.
- **Verification:** Steer clear from using documents with private info, such as your home address or school ID, when you have to verify your identity.
- **Digital footprint:** The trail of your digital footprint will follow you for the rest of your life! If someone searches your name, they can spot what you were up to ages ago! So, curate carefully.
- **Clean up:** We all hit some awkward phases. So, check old posts for anything that could be compromising and delete it. You can't erase the internet's memory, but at least you can control what's public moving forward.

- **Google yourself:** Perform a search on yourself to see what the outside world is seeing when they look you up. Delete and tweak information accordingly to ensure your safety and authenticity.
- **Screenshot evidence:** Whenever the going gets tough and friends get trolled, security breaches happen, or offensive, fake content gets out, make sure to screenshot the evidence, block offenders ASAP, report the post, and loop in trusted adults!

Common Online Threats

The web connects us to pretty much anything, including danger. Yes, it might sound harsh, but that's the unfortunate truth. Let's break down some common threats:

- **Online predators:** These mental manipulators target and exploit their victims in the most unthinkable ways. They generally start off by establishing relationships through compliments and then follow them up with inappropriate requests as soon as trust is earned. Once that happens, they will use fear and threats as a means of control. They're nothing short of pure evil! They want to isolate and silence you, so fight back by exposing them. Immediately report any uncomfortable conversations and tell a trusted adult. Those freaks need to be caught. And, absolutely never, ever agree to any offline meetups with anyone you are not well acquainted with. Safety 101!
- **Pornography:** This has been taken to a whole new level with sites such as OnlyFans, where porn is deceptively marketed as empowering. What a lie! It simply warps ideas of healthy relationships and intimacy, along with fueling low self-esteem. Immediately block suggestive

accounts and speak up. Surround yourself with messages and content that celebrate true beauty. You deserve respect.

- **Fake information:** What spreads faster than a bad rash? Fake news! Sometimes, it's tough to know what's real or not out there, but you need to learn how to separate fact from fiction. You can do this by checking the author's credibility on sites, analyzing the language used for manipulation tactics, and researching the references cited. Don't just accept, verify!

- **Phishing scams:** There's no royal Nigerian prince that's going to deposit millions of dollars into your bank account. Don't be gullible, it makes you vulnerable to fraudsters trying to steal your passwords and money. Never click on sketchy links or texts that make lottery and other far-fetched claims. If something sounds too good to be true, it usually is. Immediately delete any suspicious messages and avoid sharing any private information online.

- **Cyberbullying:** Never engage and clap back at trolls, simply block them. They're not worth your precious time. Don't let mean comments hijack your self-worth when jealousy rears its ugly head. Report any form of harassment to have these bullies removed from social platforms.

Ethical Considerations and Best Practices for Digital Behavior

Being a responsible digital citizen is not just about knowing how to navigate the uber-connected world, it's also about online ethics. I am referring to what is known as "netiquette," or good manners on the net. How exactly can you mindfully harness technology's reach while avoiding common digital fumbles?

Let's have a look at how you can decide the perfect tone and prioritize empathy because your influence online ethically impacts others too.

- Keep a cool head and avoid provoking others or engaging in inflammatory conversations.
- Respect privacy and avoid sharing personal info and pictures of others. How would you feel if your group chat gossip or karaoke shenanigans were leaked without warning? Exactly.
- Don't be spammy and scammy, and avoid sending unsolicited messages.
- When discussions get heated, stay focused and stick to the topic. It's better to be responsive and solution-driven instead of reactive and hobbling off on unproductive or unprovoked tangents.
- Skip the salty trash talk and show good sportsmanship when you're gaming online.
- Avoid trolling people in the comments. Pointless annoyance says more about you than anything else.
- If you know the answers to questions, respond! Helping someone versus just mindlessly scrolling is a lot more empowering.
- Steer clear from offensive, inappropriate language by remaining civil, intelligent, and credible.
- Never respond negatively, even to negative comments. We all have room for improvement. Reply with empathy and insightful positivity, or don't engage at all.
- Always say please and thank you, just as you would in the real world!

LEVERAGING DIGITAL TOOLS FOR SUCCESS

Let's look at how you can use this fantastic, vast digital playground to level up in life. After all, you can find resources and much more about pretty much anything out there, whether it's about math, computer sciences, or cosplay costumes.

You can hop onto simple, helpful forums or full-on classes, presented by experts, for free! There are websites, podcasts, apps, and the ever-popular YouTube, it's endless. Want to brush up on coding? CodeAcadamey or Kahn Academy will help you out. Languages? Head on over to the awesome app Duolingo. It's a knowledge rabbit hole out there!

Curiosity and an internet connection can turn you into a master of, literally, any topic. You just need to be willing and able to tap into the relevant resources. However, don't go and dabble on any sites and resources that aren't reputable. Look for hallmarks of bonafide validity. Who are the authors and organizations? Knowledge holds immense power, but application is what fortifies learning and changes lives. It's best to hunt down digital tools that also provide some hands-on learning for things, such as coding, website design, or circuit building. Applying concepts makes them stick long term.

Then, there's the power of community! Connect with like-minded people on the same learning journey through online forums and threads like Reddit. The collaboration, troubleshooting, and celebration you get from these digital tribes all help with accountability.

Online learning is not just all about subject matter; it can be harnessed for personal growth as well. Apps such as Headspace and Calm are awesome for finding some peace amid life's chaos, offering a variety of meditation and breathing exercises. Tune in to some podcasts and TED Talks for discussions and lectures on deep topics and magnificent insights to help you consume ideas from other inspirational folks.

Through continuous learning, you can transform insecurities into purpose.

Course Platforms for Personal Development

Wanna quench your curiosity, ditch those mental blocks, and boost your self-worth? Well, get ready to open your mind and say hello to the following platforms!

- **Coursera:** Great for classes, and is crafted by top international universities and companies like Google. Plus, they offer certificates too!
- **LinkedIn Learning:** Looking to boost career opportunities? LinkedIn is rife with exclusive video courses and certifications for revamping professional abilities.
- **Masterclass:** You can seriously learn songwriting from Alicia Keys herself on this celeb-led platform! Want to improve those cooking skills? Say hi to Gordon Ramsey! Because, well, why not?
- **Domestika:** This is great for upgrading hobby skills through tutorials on painting, music production, interior design, and much more!
- **Future Learn:** Here, you can choose between free or paid access to university-backed courses and even snag an accredited full degree!
- **Study.com and Khan Academy:** Two awesome platforms that let you geek out and expand knowledge across middle school, HS, and college-level academics.

- **Wondrium:** This is a "binge learning" platform, just like Netflix. It's full of documentaries that explore super niche topics, from astronomy and true crime to relationships and personal finance.
- **Creative Live:** So, you're a creative genius? Head on over to this platform and unleash your genius through broadcast classes on photography, calligraphy, baking, and, basically, any visual or crafty pursuit.
- **Alsion:** Here, you will find yourself immersed in a deep course library, covering languages, tech skills, health, and wellness. All for free, along with paid upgrades!
- **Lead Academy:** The home of many topics! From professional to hobby, they all live here with flexible pacing to suit your schedule.
- **SkillShare:** This is an extremely insightful platform that builds real-world skills in website development, social media strategy, writing, and more.
- **Shaw Academy:** Hop on over and you'll find many niche hobby and tech classes galore to choose from.
- **Mindvalley:** This is all about mindfulness, meditation, and self-healing for soothing souls. Namaste!
- **Learn from Fiverr:** Tap into tutorials on how to succeed as a digital freelancer, including marketing tactics, project management, and branding basics 101.
- **edX:** Here, you'll find a solid mixture of free and paid courses across endless academic disciplines from Ivy League schools like Oxford and Harvard.
- **Teachable:** This platform lets anyone share knowledge as creators of paid courses across infinite topics.

HANDS-ON ELEMENT: ENHANCING YOUR DIGITAL COMPETENCE

You're an official, certified digizen! It's time to put your smarts into action because learning doesn't stop here. Skills are only built when action is taken.

1. **Skill assessment:** What are you currently enjoying on the net? Perhaps, you enjoy mixing up some marvelous memes on CapCut? Maybe you enjoy refining your makeup artistry? What makes you excited to discuss with friends? Understanding your interest is your starting line.

2. **Learning plan:** It's time to come up with a good plan again! How can you fuel your passions and goals with technology? Outline all the necessary apps and tools you'll need to level up. Schedule tutorials to watch and jot down some courses you can take. Use the SMART goal method to set deadlines and keep you motivated.

3. **Safety and privacy audit:** Audit your privacy practices, update passwords so hackers are banned, double-check social media exposure, and research common online scams. This will protect your peace of mind as you keep treading that digital footprint.

4. **Responsible digizen:** You represent not only yourself but the entire digital community every time you engage online. Represent your authentic, highest self by following platform guidelines and spreading only uplifting, inclusive content. Get familiar with netiquette!

5. **Digital maintenance:** Take breaks from screen time to curb fatigue, or schedule your device updates during these breaks. Regularly do app check-ins and skill-building sessions so you stay safely on top of emerging trends too.

6. **Reflect and pivot:** Reflect on your journey and bring forth the necessary changes. Your digital path will evolve as your knowledge expands, it's not static!

Now that you understand how to optimize online tools for creativity, business, and passion projects while balancing safety, you're an official digital rockstar! So, off you go to conquer the world! Just remember to stay aligned with your values as the digital ambassador of your brand. It's all about etiquette, ethics, and keeping yourself and others safe online.

Are you ready to become even more confident, happy, and, well, "green"? I'm talking about saving the actual world! Oh yes, we're going to get our green on and delve into mastering sustainability to join the fight against environmental destruction! Sure, you're just one person so what can you really change? I say: everything!

Let's get this party started!

CHAPTER EIGHT

GOING GREEN: YOUR GUIDE TO ECO-FRIENDLY LIVING

Oh yes, folks, we have fast fashion, Amazon deliveries, and globetrotting influencers in private jets! Doesn't sustainability feel dead with so many easy, everyday choices that can trash the planet?

This generation is infamous for getting ridiculed as lazy and entitled, right? But, I say it's time to prove them wrong and glow up as leaders of sustainability! There's so much you can do from conscious shopping to political activism to ditching single-use plastics. Even the smallest daily changes can make a massive impact and that's exactly why we're going to unveil just how easy impactful green living can be. Yup, we're going to look at all of it. From food waste tragedies to fashion destruction, and even non-eco travel, you'll be a voice for change.

So, let's make this sustainable swap and see where and how you can choose Earth-first options!

UNDERSTANDING ENVIRONMENTAL IMPACT

Let's start by being real: Nobody will ever be 100% waste-free, always shop local, ditch cars, stop flying, and fully curb fossil fuel usage alone. We are here to enjoy the brilliance of life—invention, innovation, and all! It's not about perfection; it's about making better choices.

It's truly crazy to see how much damage our modern-day conveniences unleash on our planet. With the average global temperature creeping up over 1°C since industrialization rolled in, we broke the universal thermostat in just over 100 years of production. That's pretty crazy when you consider that Earth is over 4 billion years old! This environmental warming opened Pandora's box, unleashing surging wildfires with droughts, extreme weather patterns that demolish communities, and rising sea levels drowning islands and cities by feet. Our planet is, literally, screaming out for help, but we keep pushing it to the brink.

We need to eco-act together, peeps, before it's too late. We owe it to our future generations. After all, who wants their children to inherit a hot mess? We need environmental awareness through our voices and choices. So, what are the top offenders that make up this biosphere wrecking ball?

At the top of the charts, we have filthy fossil fuels. Society's little addition to gas-guzzling mobiles, plastic production, and planet-choking oil, trapping excess heat and, literally, altering our atmosphere. This contributes to rapid warming that devastates ecosystems. Then, we have all those factories popping up, requiring some serious deforestation that's robbing our wildlife and disrupting nature's balance as species are disappearing all over the world. We depend on this balance for clean air, crop pollination, medicine, and so much more. We're all responsible and dependent!

What do you think cranking up the AC does? Do the extra fracked gas and coal requirements for the extra power cross your mind? What about thoughtlessly clutching at a plastic water bottle instead of simply refilling it? Did you know that laziness contributes to this chaos? Aside from that, we need to collectively put pressure on these corporations and governments to adopt better environmental policies. I mean, seriously, this environmental negligence must end!

But, there's a bright side to this story; more leaders are waking up as generations, like this one, are rising up and speaking out. Nobody else is going to rescue humanity; it's time for you to be the change. But, the trick is that you have to be authentic with your intentions.

Daily Habits Negatively Affecting the Environment

Word has it that, apparently, it takes 3 weeks for a person to form a habit. Pretty quick, huh? And, I bet it takes longer than that to get rid of one, especially the bad ones that negatively affect you and the environment. Right?

Well, it's best that we take a look at what some of these negative habits that destroy our lovely planet look like. We need to know what to steer clear of.

- **Driving alone in gasoline-powered cars:** Having your own wheels is cool, but, unfortunately, not for the environment. Driving alone in cars contributes to air pollution and greenhouse gasses that muck around with our ecosystems and oxygen.

- **Improper disposal of cartridges and batteries:** Filled with toxic chemicals, ink cartridges and batteries pollute ecosystems and harm wildlife if proper disposal guidelines are ignored.
- **Improper disposal of plastics:** Plastic takes super-duper long to decompose. So much of it isn't disposed of properly, only to end up in our landfills and oceans, harming wildlife and ecosystems.
- **Food waste:** Food waste that ends up in landfills produces methane, a dangerously potent greenhouse gas that contributes to climate change.
- **Excessive use of paper products:** Using paper excessively contributes to deforestation, leading to significant environmental impacts like habitat loss for wildlife.
- **Inefficient electricity use:** Using excessive electricity instead of solar power or gas burns unnecessary amounts of fossil fuels, which, you know, is detrimental to our planet.
- **Soaps containing plastic microbeads:** Exfoliants that contain plastic microbeads are troublesome to filter out during sewage treatment, thus ending up in waterways and harming marine life.
- **Meat and animal product consumption:** You wanna contribute to methane production? Eating animal meat, especially from cows, produces significant amounts of methane. Not exactly the best contribution to make, right?
- **Excessive toilet flushing:** Yup, too much flushing and inefficient toilet models use massive amounts of water per flush. What a waste of such a precious resource. Literally flushed down the toilet!
- **Leaving the water running:** Leaving the faucet running while brushing your teeth, washing your face, or doing

dishes also wastes gallons of water. Not exactly what I'd call making a splash.

- **Increased electricity usage:** More screen time means more electricity consumption, which means more burning of fossil fuels. Staying up to date is cool, but what if there's no tomorrow because we're too busy caring about what others do instead of caring about the planet?
- **Unnecessary purchases:** Ah, the perks of consumerism that fuel industrial processing, pollution, and waste. That's not exactly trendy!
- **Not recycling:** Material like plastic, glass, and paper that aren't recycled properly only end up in landfills, contributing to pollution and the waste of valuable resources. Everything needs a second chance in life, right?
- **Online shopping:** Yes, it's convenient. Yes, it's fun. And, yes, it contributes to emissions from delivery trucks and packaging waste. So, remember, you're not just online shopping for a product, you're contributing to greenhouse gas emissions too. That's, most certainly, not a bargain!

These are just a couple of examples of how our actions can negatively impact our planet. We need to become more aware of the impacts of our choices to be able to make better ones for a healthier, cleaner tomorrow.

The Role of Individuals in Combating Climate Change

So, what's your role in tackling this whole climate change situation we're finding ourselves in? You know, we all have a part to play in this when it comes to changing the trajectory; it starts with taking responsibility for our own actions and choices.

Climate change isn't this far-off abstract concept that only affects polar bears and other extinct creatures. It's a real, tangible thing! It's a serious threat to our planet, communities, and way of life. What's even more crazy than this? We're all contributing to it in some way or the other, whether you realize it or not. That's a scary thought to think.

Every time we hop into our cars for a solo drive, leave the lights on when we're not in the room, brush our teeth and leave the water running, or sip from our plastic water bottles, we're only adding to this saga! Sure, you might think it's not a big deal in the scheme of grander things but multiply your action by billions of people across the globe. The result? It adds up at the speed of light and our planet is battling to sustain us.

The good news? If you're part of the problem, you can also be part of the solution. It's not an overnight lifestyle overhaul. Let's be realistic. It's about being mindful and making small, conscious decisions that will add up, contributing to a greener future over time. Take transportation as an example. Rather than grabbing your car keys, go for a walk, ride a bike, carpool with friends or coworkers, or take public transport instead. You'll be cutting emissions down to size! Plus, fresh air, more exercise, and good company are great added extras. Let's not overlook the savings on gas either.

When it comes to home sweet home, there are plenty of things you can do that'll make a difference. For instance, make sure your light bulbs are energy-efficient LEDs, unplug unused electronics, adjust your thermostats, and recycle your waste. See, easy as pie! These small changes will give you an even smaller carbon footprint. Individual actions are great! But, for serious change, you need to think bigger. How can you get your community involved? Can you join any local initiatives or support organizations that promote sustainability or spread the word by speaking up about it on social platforms? Of course, you can!

The more you show you care, the more people will care, and the bigger momentum is created for lasting change. It's like a ripple effect! So, walk the walk and talk the talk. It's so much more than just doing the right thing for the planet. It's about doing the right thing for ourselves, each other, and future generations.

PRACTICING SUSTAINABLE LIVING

So, are you ready to become an eco-warrior and make a difference for our planet? Here are some straightforward, practical tips to bring those green vibes into your daily life:

- **Sure, it's convenient to have a car, but at what costs when you consider the environment?** Did you know you don't have to drive solo everywhere? You can walk, scooter, bike, or even skateboard wherever you need to go. Plus, it's an awesome way to get in that must-have regular dose of daily physical activity.
- **If distance is a problem, hop onto public transport or carpool with your squad to help Mother Earth.** It's cheaper for everyone and reduces traffic. What a win-win scenario, right?
- **Wanna save some energy? Hunt down all those sneaky air leaks around doors and windows around the home.** Seal them up and don't forget to unplug unused electronics to sidestep those energy "phantoms."
- **Reduce your meat consumption!** Look, I'm not saying go all vegan. Simply go meatless at least a day a week. This little change can make a significant change when it comes

to your carbon footprint. Plus, you can explore some new plant-based dishes!

- **Read the fine print on those food labels.** Keep your eyes peeled for local and organic products, and steer clear of the overly processed stuff. You can even take it a step further and start your own backyard or windowsill veggie garden!
- **Cut down on food waste by using the scraps in creative ways, getting smart with your grocery choices, and composting.** You'll do your wallet and the planet a solid.
- **Wave bye-bye to toxic chemicals that spill over into the environment and make space for greener cleaning.** Make the switch to eco-friendly cleaning goodies or whip up your own magic brews to turn your humble abode into a sparkling palace.
- **Be a green teen!** Get everyone on board and chat about climate change and going green with your family and friends.
- **Take action and make your voice heard by signing petitions urging for changes that protect the environment.** Every signature counts!

Remember, every small change adds up and every little bit helps. By making simple changes in your daily life, you're actively becoming part of the solution.

Reduce, Reuse, and Recycle Effectively

I'd say the time is right to dive into the three R's: reduce, reuse, and recycle. And, trust me, it's way easier than you might think.

Reduce

Reduce simply means that you cut down on the amount of stuff you use and chuck away. The best place to start is by being mindful and thinking twice before you buy stuff. Only buy what you need, especially when it comes to food! And, unsubscribe to any junk mail because all it is, well, is junk!

When you're out and about hustling, avoid unnecessary added extras, like plastic takeout utensils and straws. Pack your lunch in waste-free reusable containers instead of plastic wrap or one-use chuckaway bags.

Reuse

It's all about giving items a second life instead of just tossing them into the trash can. Do you have clothes, appliances, and furniture you no longer need? Donate it to second-hand stores or nonprofit organizations. You know, one man's trash is another man's treasure! Switch from disposable to reusable where and when you can, like single-use water bottles versus reusable ones, disposable razors versus reusable ones, or paper napkins versus cloth ones. It all adds up over time!

Recycle

Sort your waste and send it to where it can be processed into new products. Familiarize yourself with what gets recycled—you'll be pleasantly surprised, trust me! Another pro tip is to hold onto glass jars and ice cream containers for future use. It'll save you some cash on purchasing additional Tupperware. Plus, take your own reusable shopping bags on your hauls. Always choose and use minimal packaging.

Be the change and set an example; reduce, reuse, and recycle!

ADVOCACY AND COMMUNITY INVOLVEMENT

Take your passion for the planet, start advocating for environmental issues, and ensure your voice is heard loud and proud!

You gotta get out there, get informed, and be educated to spread the word. After all, knowledge is power. Take time and explore trusted resources to get the deets on environmental issues. It doesn't matter what you're into—whether it's tackling climate change, reducing plastic pollution, protecting wildlife and natural spaces, or promoting sustainable agriculture—there are tons of incredible organizations out there with valid info. Check out the *Rise Above Plastics Activist Toolkit* from the Surfrider Foundation for some excellent tips on creating positive change in your community by curbing single-use plastics. You don't just wanna go green because it's trendy; you ought to go green to make a tangible impact!

If climate change is your big vibe, hop on over to Citizens' Climate Education and the Climate Reality Project for some climate change solutions. You can even consider starting your own local movement to connect with like-minded folks and work together toward a common goal: saving the planet. Yeah! Lean into the power of strength in numbers!

Perhaps you're into wildlife and protecting precious land like forests. Educate yourself about all the ins and outs of developmental threats, natural resource exploitation, pollution, and climate change—all issues with serious impacts that need some standing up against for future generations. Check out resources like The Wilderness Society for some tips and resources on how to get started. Do you have green fingers? Then, sustainable agriculture should top your list of interests. Beyond Pesticides Action of the Week is a good bet that provides one impactful action a week that you can take to have your voice heard on policies that are harmful to the environment and our health. We do need a more eco-friendly food system!

You don't have to explode onto the scene and go big from the get-go. Keep it close to home if you want because advocating for a more livable, safe local community is just as important. Explore your local area and government resources, such as The Transportation Toolkit, to get the latest lowdown on major infrastructure projects and see how you can dive into the action. You can get so much information, like flowcharts, timelines, and more, that breaks down the complexities of planning, empowering you to get involved and get your voice out there.

Once you have a solid grasp of the issues that hit home, spread the word and engage others. Have meaningful convos to influence your peeps for the better. Share what you've learned and discuss your plans and goals to inspire them to care about our planet too. Your conversations are also contributions. Ready to amp up your advocacy? Hit up online petitions and writing campaigns to let your elected officials know that you demand real action on environmental issues.

With just a couple of clicks, you can join organizations like Environmental Defence, giving a voice to passionate, young people just like you who are committed to a sustainable future. Why stop there? Join local environmental groups in your area. They'll be thrilled to have you onboard! On local levels, you get to plan events, attend meetings, and rub shoulders with like-minded folks to create real change. Heck, consider running for office yourself! Sure, it sounds a bit out there, but there are plenty of organizations out there that want to support young, environmentally-minded candidates. Just imagine the change you could make by bringing your decision-making prowess to the table with the intention of prioritizing the health of our planet and its people.

Of course, there are plenty of fun and creative ways to get involved. Arrange a beach clean-up with your friends or start a sustainable school garden. There are so many options. You can even start a sustainable fashion swap circle that encourages folks to make eco-friendly fashion choices and reduce textile waste.

You also don't have to just pick and stick to one issue. There are so many possibilities and you'll certainly find more than one that aligns with your passions. You just need to get out there and explore what works best for you and your unique skills and interests. Maybe you're a gifted writer, social media guru, or a smooth-talking public speaker, there's a spot for you to fight for a greener, more sustainable tomorrow.

Don't feel overwhelmed, but, if you do, reach out for guidance and support to organizations like Earth Share for some solid guidance and connections. You're not alone in this battle; there are plenty of young folks sharing your passion and commitment.

Remember, stay informed, stay connected, stay passionate, and stay connected to your vision for a greener future.

Community-Based Environmental Initiatives

Brooklyn-based freelance writer and founder of the *Sustaining Life* blog, Faye Lessler, beautifully summarized the following initiatives, making it easier for you to reach out and make a change (n.d.).

A Growing Culture

- Supports smallholder farmers and agroecological innovation
- Facilitates farmer-to-farmer exchange and research
- *Get involved:* Follow on Instagram or donate to the cause

Native American Traditional Food Systems (NATIFS)

- Focuses on re-establishing Native foodways
- Works toward a new food system for Native communities
- *Get involved:* Donate or purchase the co-founder's cookbook

Cultural Survival

- Indigenous peoples protect 80% of Earth's biodiversity
- Fights for Indigenous rights and self-determination
- *Ways to get involved:* Contribute to storytelling, donate, and boycott companies

Fashion Revolution

- A global movement for a fairer fashion industry
- Hosts events like Fashion Revolution Week
- *Get involved:* Participate in #WhoMadeMyClothes, write letters, donate

Earthjustice

- Largest environmental law organization in the U.S.
- Protects laws for a healthy planet
- *Get involved:* Donate, join campaigns

School Girls Unite

- Promotes girls' education and leadership
- Education as a solution for poverty and climate change
- *Get involved:* Sign up for newsletter, share petition, donate

Natural Resources Defense Council (NRDC)

- Works to safeguard the earth and its resources
- Collaborates with various stakeholders
- *Get involved:* Donate, join campaigns

American Forests

- Focuses on forest restoration and policy
- Planted over 50 million trees
- *Get involved:* Donate, gift a tree, shop partner brands

Conservation International

- Protects land, marine, and coastal areas worldwide
- Works with governments and businesses
- *Get involved:* Donate, take pledge, read tips for greener living

One Percent For the Planet

- Global network for environmental action
- Members commit 1% of profits to environmental causes
- *Get involved:* Become a member, support member brands

National Audubon Society

- Protects birds and their habitats
- Works with scientists, lawmakers, and activists
- *Get involved:* Donate, become a member, join campaigns

Jane Goodall Institute

- Protects chimpanzees and promotes wildlife conservation
- Engages global community for collective action
- *Get involved:* Donate, become a chimp guardian, shop products

Sierra Club

- Advocates for clean air, water, and wildlife conservation
- Organizes outdoor activities and campaigns
- *Get involved:* Join treks, add your voice, donate

5 Gyres Institute

- Fights against plastic pollution in oceans
- Works with global businesses and activists
- *Get involved:* Donate, pledge to refuse plastic, become an ambassador

Nature Conservancy

- Protects lands and waters worldwide
- Collaborates for climate change solutions
- *Get involved:* Volunteer, donate

Blue Sphere Foundation

- Safeguards oceans through action and art
- Focuses on biodiversity protection and eco-tourism
- *Get involved:* Donate, join expeditions

350.org

- Mobilizes for climate change solutions
- Focuses on clean energy and carbon reduction
- *Get involved:* Join local groups, start your own group, donate

Lonely Whale Foundation

- Creates environmental change through community action
- Focuses on plastic pollution and eco-education
- *Get involved:* Check campaigns, donate

Cool Effect

- Reduces carbon emissions through community support
- Funds various carbon-reducing projects
- *Get involved:* Donate to campaigns, purchase offsets

Earth Guardians

- Empowers youth for environmental activism
- Focuses on practical climate change solutions
- *Get involved:* Check the action center, attend events, donate

Greenpeace

- Advocates for environmental protection
- Conducts activism against climate change
- *Get involved:* Join local groups, follow journalism sites, donate

Project Drawdown

- Provides solutions to reverse global warming
- Educates and supports effective initiatives
- *Get involved:* Read their book, attend events, donate

Regenerative Agriculture Alliance

- Committed to a regenerative future
- Advocates for Indigenous agricultural practices
- *Get involved:* Donate

Fibershed

- Promotes regional and regenerative fiber systems
- Educates about decentralized textile systems
- *Get involved:* Donate, attend events

Regeneration International

- Promotes regenerative food and land management
- Collaborates with international partners
- *Get involved:* Join the network, attend events, donate

Sustainable Harvest International

- Empowers farmers through sustainable farming
- Fights against hunger, poverty, and deforestation
- *Get involved:* Travel, attend events, volunteer, donate

The Soil Association

- Advocates for healthy and sustainable food systems
- Certifies sustainable products and campaigns
- *Get involved:* Donate, become a member, volunteer

HANDS-ON ELEMENT: EMBRACING SUSTAINABLE PRACTICES IN DAILY LIFE

Time for some actionable steps to incorporate eco-friendly practices into your daily routine! We'll break it down into easy-to-follow steps that will help you become a sustainability maverick in no time!

1. Personal environmental audit:

A. Take a moment to assess your current lifestyle. Think about how much energy you use, how much waste you produce, and how you get from "A" to "B" daily.

B. Identify areas where you could make more eco-friendly choices. Maybe you can cut down on single-use plastics, or find creative ways to save water and electricity.

2. Setting eco-friendly goals:

A. Set some small, realistic goals to improve your environmental impact based on your audit. Make them specific and realistic. For example, aim to cut your household waste in half or commit to using public transportation more often.

B. Break these goals into smaller steps. It's easier to make progress when you tackle things one step at a time!

3. Implement sustainable practices:

A. Start simple and use reusable bags, water bottles, and containers. Easy does it, so work your way up to bigger changes as soon as you get comfy with the smaller ones.

B. Encourage a recycling program at home, or switch to energy-efficient electronics and appliances.

4. Educate yourself and others:

A. Never stop learning about environmental issues and sustainable living. There are ample resources out there, like books, documentaries, and reliable websites that'll keep you up to date with current events.

B. Spread the love and share what you learn with your friends, family, and community. The magic will rub off and you'll inspire them to make changes too!

5. Community involvement:

A. Get out there and get involved by joining a community clean-up, helping plant trees, or attending sustainability workshops.

B. Speak up! You can make a huge impact by raising awareness and encouraging others to take action.

6. Eco-conscious consumption:

A. Always be mindful of your purchases. Look for products from eco-friendly and ethical brands, and think twice about how sustainable they are.

B. Before you make a purchase, ask yourself, "Do I really need it?" Quality over quantity!

7. Reflect and adjust:

A. Reflect on your progress, celebrate the changes you've made, and think about areas where there's room for improvement.

B. Remember, it's okay to make mistakes, nobody's perfect. Think of your mistakes as learning opportunities to keep growing. It's about progress, not perfection.

8. Long-term commitment:

A. Sustainability isn't a short-term trend. It's a lifestyle change. Stay informed and keep looking for ways to reduce, reuse, recycle, and improve your impact.

B. And, don't forget; every small change you make helps protect our planet for tomorrow's generations.

We've covered a lot of green ground, from simple everyday changes to full-on community involvement, inspiring you to make a difference today for a better tomorrow.

It's not about being perfect; it's about making better choices and progressing to live more sustainably. Every action counts! So, ditch those single-use plastics, carpool with friends, or speak up for what you care about. Become part of this growing movement that invests every day in every little way toward a brighter, greener future.

The planet needs you! So become the change you want to see!

Look how far you've come! From diving right into the world of personal finance and discovering true life's passions to cultivating meaningful relationships and prioritizing personal growth and development. Oh yes, we've covered some solid ground and made some serious progress in your journey toward independent adulthood!

Hey, let's not overlook those epic life skill essentials we've picked apart. Who knew grocery shopping is a fine art and basic car maintenance is a must-have? Then, we stepped into career planning, eco-friendly living, and navigating the digital world too! How empowering! As we come to the conclusion of this epic, transformative adventure, take a breath and just look at how far you've come and how much you've learned. You started out as an eager beaver, curious to learn and ready to soak up knowledge like a sponge. And, now? Just look at you in all your glory, armed with strategies, insights, and practical tips to take on the world and live your best life possible. And, do you know what's even more exciting? This is just the beginning of many great things headed your way.

One thing you must not only realize but also embrace is the fact that learning and personal growth are not an overnight thing; they're a lifelong pursuit. They have to be in order for you to improve and evolve, experiencing the best of what life has to offer. After all, if you don't grow, what happens? You wither away! So, keep challenging yourself every step of the way as you move forward. Don't be afraid to step outside your comfort zone or, shall I say, comfort illusion. Try new things, explore new places, meet new people, and never stop being curious. You'll never have all the answers in life. Nobody does. So, get comfy with the unknown and life's ups, downs, successes, and failures. They're not a measure of your worth; they are lessons in disguise and you have to take what you learned from these moments to level up. They're not roadblocks; they simply redirect you toward growth, development, and opportunity.

You know that sharing is caring. Share what you've learned with others, it's the ultimate power move! Be a role model, mentor, helping hand, and source of inspiration for others. Be a testament to success, showing what a little bit of hard work, willingness to learn, and determination with a good dose of resilience can produce. Anything is possible! If you can dream it, with some action, you can do it!

Reflect on the key messages in this book and, remember, that success isn't about perfection and achieving your goals; it's about the awesome, fulfilled person you become in the process. It's about resilience, grit, a growth mindset, and some serious life skills that will serve you well. It's about acceptance as well, flaws and all, to be able to step into your authentic self.

You deserve healthy relationships, a fulfilling career, and a life filled with meaning and purpose. This might be the end of the book, but it's a new chapter in your life. Trust in yourself and your abilities. You undoubtedly have what it takes to achieve anything you set out to do. It doesn't matter how big or small your dreams are, just don't let fear and doubt hold you back from reaching your full potential.

Remember, life is not one big, fat straight line. There are going to be detours, setbacks, and mistakes that will change your course along the way. Just keep your cool and stick to your values and passions. Keep pushing forward, even when times seem dark. They won't last forever, I promise. Trust that every single experience, whether good or bad, is an opportunity for you to expand your greatness. You're gifted and talented, so share it with the world in your unique way. Be the change instead of waiting for others. You're a trendsetter and a smart swaggy teen, not a follower.

Look, let's be honest: Learning and growing isn't always easy. But, as much as it can be a pain in the rear at times, acknowledge the incredible work you've put in and celebrate how far you've come. As long as you show up, day after day, and are ready and willing to take on new challenges, you'll be unstoppable.

If you've enjoyed this journey as much as I have and found value in the lessons, insights, and strategies shared amid these pages, take a moment and leave a review. Check-in and let me know how things are panning out. Your honest feedback will not only offer me great insight as an author to grow and improve but will also be an inspiration and help spread the message of personal growth and development. There are so many awesome teens, just like you, ready to take on the world. Together, we can create a community that inspires others to take control and chase their dreams with passion, purpose, and competence.

However, just remember, the skills and knowledge you gained from this book are merely the tip of the iceberg. It's in your hands now. Take action and apply what you have learned, pushing yourself to new heights in good time.

You're never alone! Reach out for guidance and support in times of confusion and overwhelm. Asking for help has never been a weakness; it only serves to further empower you. Lean on your peeps and celebrate with them as you achieve milestones. Also, be there for them, relationships are a two-way street. Yup, it's all about give and take. Whether it's through volunteering, mentoring, or simply being a positive presence in your community, know that every small action has the power to create a ripple effect of change.

Get out there and make your mark in the world! The path of personal growth and development is surely a great one. And, I'm honored to have been a part of yours! I can't wait to hear about all the incredible things you'll accomplish.

Until our paths cross again, keep shining—the future is yours for the taking!

You know that you're never alone, but there are teens out there who don't feel like that right now. Why not reach out a helping hand and help them discover these crucial skills?

Simply by sharing your honest opinion of this book and a little about what you found here, you'll point new readers in the direction of the guidance they're looking for.

LET'S HEAR FROM YOU!

Thank you so much for your support. You have a thrilling future ahead of you: Enjoy every moment.

Scan the QR code below

REFERENCES

"30 Best Adulting Quotes to Make You Feel Better About Growing Up." The Grown-Up School. Last modified March 22, 2023. https://thegrownupschool. com/adulting-quotes-to-make-you-feel-better-about-growing-up/.

A beginner's guide to choosing the right credit card. (n.d.). Affiliate Site Masters. https://affiliatesitemasters.com/a-beginners-guide-to-choosing-the-right-credit-card/?

Antaya, M. (n.d.). *Communicating with empathy.* Eclectic Communications. https:// www.eclectic.ca/resources/blog/communicating-empathy

Are you prepared for a disaster? (n.d.). Johns Hopkins Medicine. https://www. hopkinsmedicine.org/health/wellness-and-prevention/are-you-prepared-for-a-disaster

Belliveau, E. (2023, December 12). *Six easy ways to get involved in climate action.* Environmental Defence. https://environmentaldefence.ca/2023/12/12/six-easy-ways-to-get-involved-in-climate-action/

Berry, I. (2021, September 21). *Top 10 ways to live more sustainably.* Sustainability Mag. https://sustainabilitymag.com/top10/top-10-ways-live-more-sustainably

Beyond the CV: Showcasing your skills and experience in creative ways. (2023, June 22). Pentasia. https://www.pentasia.com/blogs/beyond-the-cv-showcasing-your-skills-and-experience-in-creative-ways/

Blancaflor, M. (2022, January 19). *8 Tips and tricks for finding a great travel deal.* The Points Guy. https://thepointsguy.com/guide/tips-for-finding-travel-deals/

Botros, A., & Snyder, K. (2024, March 1). *A simple guide that shows which savings account might be the best for you.* Fortune. https://fortune.com/recommends/banking/types-of-savings-accounts/

Bridging Freedom. (2022, July 12). *How to teach your kids online safety.* Bridging Freedom. https://www.bridgingfreedom.org/online-safety/?

Brown, A. (n.d.). *The importance of a passport: Why is it so necessary for traveling?* Drift Travel Magazine. https://drifttravel.com/the-importance-of-a-passport-why-is-it-so-necessary-for-traveling/

Brubaker, A. (2022, June 1). *Choosing a career path after high school.* Connections Academy. https://www.connectionsacademy.com/support/resources/article/5-ways-help-high-school-students-pick-careers/

Buchwald, N. (2023, June 3). *How to let go of the expectations of others.* Manhattan

Mental Health Counseling. https://manhattanmentalhealthcounseling.com/how-to-let-go-of-the-expectations-of-others/

Build a good credit score with these 5 habits. (n.d.). Easyfinancial. https://www.easyfinancial.com/academy/blog/build-a-good-credit-score-with-these-5-habits?

Bulit-Gordon, T. (2023, September 10). *The importance of mental and emotional well-being.* Institute of Core Energetics. https://www.coreenergetics.org/the-importance-of-mental-and-emotional-well-being/?

Calming anxiety. (n.d.). Proulx Foundation. https://proulxfoundation.org/calming-anxiety/?gad_source=1%E2%A6%81&%E2%A6%81gclid

Can you travel without a passport? (n.d.). Handy Visas. https://www.handyvisas.com/faq/can-you-travel-without-a-passport/

Capecchi, S. (2022, June 8). *Mindfulness for teens: How it works, benefits, & 11 exercises to try.* Choosing Therapy. https://www.choosingtherapy.com/mindfulness-for-teens/

Car maintenance checklist: 9 Essential steps that anyone can do. (n.d.). Canadadrives. https://www.canadadrives.ca/blog/maintenance/car-maintenance-checklist-essentials

Carpages. (n.d.). *How to buy your first car: A comprehensive guide.* Carpages Blog. https://www.carpages.ca/blog/how-to-buy-your-first-car/

Chauhan, S. (2023, June 5). *Embrace your individuality, embrace your uniqueness, be authentic, and join the exceptional 1%.* LinkedIn. https://www.linkedin.com/pulse/embrace-your-individuality-uniqueness-authentic-join-1-%D6%86%D6%85%D5%BC%C9%A8%C7%9F-%C6%88%C9%A6%C7%9F%CA%8A%C9%A6%C7%9F%D5%BC/

Chen, J. (2023, October 12). *Investing for beginners: A guide to assets.* Investopedia. https://www.investopedia.com/articles/basics/11/3-s-simple-investing.asp

College Money Matters. (2021, July 13). *Federal student loans are for students of all incomes.* College Money Matters. https://collegemoneymatters.org/federal-student-loans-are-for-students-of-all-incomes/

College Money Matters. (2021, July 6). *How do student loans work?* College Money Matters. https://collegemoneymatters.org/how-do-student-loans-work/

CollegeNP. (2023, April 17). *Effective time management tips for students: Balancing study with other commitments.* CollegeNP. https://www.collegenp.com/article/effective-time-management-tips-for-students-balancing-study-with-other-commitments/

Cozma, I. (2023, October 23). *Values, passion, or purpose — Which should guide your career?* Harvard Business Review. https://hbr.org/2023/10/values-passion-or-purpose-which-should-guide-your-career

CTN. (2022, March 1). *14 Ways the internet improves our lives.* Community Tech Network. https://communitytechnetwork.org/blog/14-ways-the-internet-improves-our-lives/

Cultural sensitivity: A traveler's guide to learning and respecting local customs and cultures. (n.d.). Viavii. https://viavii.com/blog/cultural-sensitivity-a-travelers-guide-to-learning-and-respecting-local-customs-and-cultures#:

Daugherty, G. (2023, December 21). *How to save money for your big financial goals.* Investopedia. https://www.investopedia.com/how-to-save-money-4589942#:

Del Rosario, T. M. (2022, October 27). *The power of communication in a relationship.* Healing Collective Therapy. https://www.healingcollectivetherapy.com/resources/power-of-communication-in-relationship

Dillon, A. (n.d.). *Digital learning resources.* Study.com. https://study.com/academy/lesson/what-are-digital-learning-resources-overview-examples.html#:

Discover. (2023, February 21). *How do you pay for a health emergency or major repairs if you haven't saved the money? Here are some common sources of financing if you don't have an emergency fund.* Personal Loans. https://www.discover.com/personal-loans/resources/major-expenses/planning-unexpected-expenses/

Eby, K. (2019, January 9). *The essential guide to writing S.M.A.R.T. goals.* Smartsheet. https://www.smartsheet.com/blog/essential-guide-writing-smart-goals

Emotional intelligence. (n.d.). Psychology Today. https://www.psychologytoday.com/ca/basics/emotional-intelligence

Environmental awareness. (n.d.). Heart Water. https://drinkheartwater.com/blog/environmental-awareness

ESoft Skills. (n.d.). *Strategies for clear and compassionate communication.* ESoft Skills. https://esoftskills.com/healthcare/strategies-for-clear-and-compassionate-communication/

FamilyDoctor. (2023, March). *Nutrition: How to make healthier food choices.* Familydoctor.org. https://familydoctor.org/nutrition-how-to-make-healthier-food-choices/

Fifteen top tips for everyday sustainable living. (n.d.). David Suzuki Foundation. https://davidsuzuki.org/living-green/fifteen-top-tips-for-everyday-sustainable-living/?gad_source=1%E2%A6%81&%E2%A6%81gclid   Fleximize. (n.d.). *Adapting communication styles to different audiences.* Fleximize. https://fleximize.com/articles/000592/communication-styles

Frerichs, B. (2021, March 2). *10 Benefits of an internship & mentor program.* Chief Industries. https://chiefind.com/10-benefits-of-an-internship-mentor-program/

GoHenry. (2023, January 9). *Budgeting for teens: A guide for parents and teenagers.* GoHenry. https://www.gohenry.com/uk/blog/financial-education/how-to-teach-your-teenager-about-budgeting

Goldman, A. (2023, May 30). *Investing 101 for beginners.* Wealthsimple. https://www.wealthsimple.com/en-ca/learn/investing-basics#basics_of_investing_in_stocks

GSAM. (2023, September 25). *7 tips for budgeting on a fluctuating income.* GetSmarterAboutMoney. https://www.getsmarteraboutmoney.ca/learning-path/budgeting/7-tips-for-budgeting-on-a-fluctuating-income/

Gupta, S. (2023, May 8). *What is self-worth?* Verywell Mind. https://www.verywellmind.com/what-is-self-worth-6543764

Hammoud, M. (2022, February 13). *The ABCs of clear communication.* LinkedIn. https://www.linkedin.com/pulse/abcs-clear-communication-mohamed-hammoud/

Hannahxdee. (2022, August 22). *Getting your first apartment: A guide for young adults by a young adult.* ToughNickel. https://toughnickel.com/real-estate/Getting-Your-First-Apartment-A-Guide-For-Young-Adults-by-a-Young-Adult

Hattox, A. (2023, August 21). *What makes a good resume? 15 Tips & tricks.* The Shutterstock Blog. https://www.shutterstock.com/blog/resume-tips-and-tricks?

Hayward, L. (n.d.). *How to create a realistic travel budget that actually works.* BudgetBakers. https://budgetbakers.com/create-realistic-travel-budget/

Herrity, J. (2023, February 27). *9 Tips to improve your emotional intelligence.* Indeed. https://www.indeed.com/career-advice/career-development/how-to-improve-emotional-intelligence

Herrity, J. (2023, March 11). *Five steps to learn new skills.* Indeed. https://www.indeed.com/career-advice/career-development/learn-new-skills

How to choose a career path as a teenager. (2022, October 26). Spikeview. https://www.spikeview.com/advice-for-teens-choosing-career-path/

How to file your federal taxes. (2024, January 4). Usa.gov. https://www.usa.gov/file-taxes

How to lower your grocery bill. (n.d.). Easyfinancial. https://www.easyfinancial.com/academy/blog/how-to-lower-your-grocery-bill?gclid

How to manage anxiety and fear. (n.d.). Mental Health Foundation. https://www.mentalhealth.org.uk/explore-mental-health/publications/how-overcome-anxiety-and-fear

How to repair a flat tire with a safe, permanent fix. (n.d.). Tech Tire Repair Solutions. https://techtirerepairs.com/flat-tire-how-to-safely-fix/

How to set career goals. (n.d.). Hays. https://www.hays.com.au/career-advice/career-development/setting-career-goals

Indeed. (2022, December 1). *8 Reasons for a career shift and how to make the change.* Indeed. https://ca.indeed.com/career-advice/career-development/reasons-for-career-shift

Irwin, D. (2011, November 22). *Passion over profit: How to get past pressure to pursue prestigious job*. Black Enterprise. https://www.blackenterprise.com/passion-over-profit-how-to-get-past-the-career-pressure/

John Soules Foods. (n.d.). *Cooking tips for beginners*. John Soules Foods. https://www.johnsoulesfoods.com/blog/cooking-tips-for-beginners/

Karasik, C. S. (2020, January 9). *The 5 basic cooking techniques that every healthy chef should master*. Well+Good. https://www.wellandgood.com/basic-cooking-skills/

Kuczynskirf. (2016, July 8). *Everyone has a role in the fight against climate change*. Young African Leaders Initiative. https://yali.state.gov/climate-change-everyone-has-a-role/

Larkin, E. (2022, November 21). *10 Things to do daily to be more organized*. The Spruce. https://www.thespruce.com/be-more-organized-on-daily-basis-2648474

Leading Effectively. (2023, February 8). *How to tackle difficult conversations*. Center for Creative Leadership. https://www.ccl.org/articles/leading-effectively-articles/5-steps-for-tackling-tough-conversations/

Lessler, F. (n.d.). *35 Environmental organizations and nonprofits for a sustainable future (List and ways you can get involved)*. Green Dreamer. https://www.greendreamer.com/journal/environmental-organizations-nonprofits-for-a-sustainable-future

Lucyna. (2021, October 19). *16 Best online course platforms for self-development*. Europe Language Jobs. https://www.europelanguagejobs.com/blog/16-best-online-course-platforms-for-self-development

Macapinlac, M. (n.d.). *How to express yourself verbally: 13 quick tips*. Social Confidence Mastery. https://socialconfidencemastery.com/how-to-express-yourself-verbally/

Magid, L. (2022, October 19). *11 Practical internet safety tips for keeping kids and teens safe online*. Amazon. https://www.aboutamazon.com/news/devices/internet-safety-for-kids-teens

Marcus, L. (2014, March 28). *Every single thing you need to know about renting your first apartment*. Teen Vogue. https://www.teenvogue.com/story/how-to-rent-an-apartment

MBO Partners. (2022, May 5). *5 Ways to keep your job skills and knowledge current*. MBO Partners. https://www.mbopartners.com/blog/how-manage-small-business/how-to-keep-your-skills-and-knowledge-current-and-why-it-matters1/

McCall, M. (2023, August 9). *Landlord-tenant law*. FindLaw. https://www.findlaw.com/realestate/landlord-tenant-law.html#:

Milano, S. (2020, November 10). *Choosing a career for young teenagers*. Chron. https://work.chron.com/choosing-career-young-teenagers-14040.html

Mind Tools. (n.d.). *7 Tips for effective file management*. MindTools. https://www.mindtools.com/ahjudzv/7-tips-for-effective-file-management

MoneyAndStuff.info. (n.d.). *Sample monthly budget for teens*. https://fndusa.org/wp-content/uploads/2015/06/SampleBudgetforTeens.pdf

Mydoh. (2021, December 22). *Budgeting for teens: How to budget and tips for parents*. Mydoh. https://www.mydoh.ca/learn/money-101/money-basics/budgeting-101-a-guide-for-parents-and-teenagers/

NHS. (2022, November 22). *8 Tips for healthy eating*. NHS. https://www.nhs.uk/live-well/eat-well/how-to-eat-a-balanced-diet/eight-tips-for-healthy-eating/

Olsen, I. M. (2023, August 15). *How to express yourself better in 7 steps*. Convey Clearly. http://conveyclearly.com/2023/08/15/how-to-express-yourself-better-in-7-steps/

Palmateer, J. (2017, November 7). *Are today's teenagers less prepared for adulthood than previous generations?* Parent Today. https://www.parenttoday.org/are-todays-teenagers-are-less-prepared-for-adulthood-than-previous-generations/

Pangestu, D. (n.d.). *7 Steps to saving money in an emergency fund*. My Money Coach. https://www.mymoneycoach.ca/blog/saving-emergency-fund.html

Paycheck taxes - Federal, state & local withholding. (2017, June 14). H&R Block. https://www.hrblock.com/tax-center/filing/personal-tax-planning/paycheck-taxes/

Perry, E. (2022, February 11). *8 Ways to overcome self-doubt once and for all*. BetterUp. https://www.betterup.com/blog/overcoming-self-doubt

Pettit, K. (2022, September 7). *How to become a more effective environmental advocate*. EarthShare. https://www.earthshare.org/how-to-become-a-more-effective-environmental-advocate/

Ragland, L. (2023, September 12). *Ways to manage stress*. WebMD. https://www.webmd.com/balance/stress-management/stress-management

Rainey, C. (2013, April 2). *10 Ways to build trust through communication*. 850 Business Magazine. https://www.850businessmagazine.com/10-ways-to-build-trust-through-communication/

Reduce, reuse, recycle. (n.d.). Turn Back the Tide. https://www.turnbackthetide.ca/taking-action/households/waste/reduce-reuse-recycle.shtml

Rickardsson, J. (n.d.). *Effective communication strategies for building and improving relationships*. 29K. https://29k.org/article/effective-communication-strategies-for-building-and-improving-relationships

Rinkesh. (n.d.). *15 Daily habits of human beings that are slowly killing the environment*. Conserve Energy Future. https://www.conserve-energy-future.com/daily-habits-human-beings-that-killing-environment.php

Riopel, L. (2020, January 30). *7 Most effective self-esteem tools and activities*. Positive

Psychology. https://positivepsychology.com/self-esteem-tools-activities/

Rohrbeck, T. (2022, September 2). *Digital citizenship: Digital etiquette.* Dalian American International School. https://daischina.libguides.com/digitalcitizen ship/digitaletiquette

Ryan, A. (2020, May 28). *Tips for your young adult and their 1st apartment.* Simply Family Magazine. https://simplyfamilymagazine.com/tips-for-your-young-adult-and-their-1st-apartment

Sato, G. (2023, January 25). *What's the difference between state and federal income tax?* Experian. https://www.experian.com/blogs/ask-experian/difference-between-state-and-federal-income-tax/

Saxena, S. (2022, May 3). *Self-doubt: What it is, signs, & how to overcome.* Choosing Therapy. https://www.choosingtherapy.com/self-doubt/

Segal, J., Smith, M., Robinson, L., & Boose, G. (2024, January 11). *Nonverbal communication and body language.* HelpGuide. https://www.helpguide.org/arti cles/relationships-communication/nonverbal-communication.htm

6 Tips on choosing the right travel insurance. (2023, February 27). Uniglobe Carefree Travel. https://www.uniglobecarefreetravel.com/blog/6-tips-on-choosing-the-right-travel-insurance

Social media tips for kids and teens. (2023, June 23). CHOC. https://health.choc.org/handout/social-media-tips-for-kids-and-teens/

Solaiman, M. (2023, August 9). *Annual health checkups for teens.* Mayo Clinic. https://www.mayoclinichealthsystem.org/hometown-health/speaking-of-health/add-health-checkup-to-teens-back-to-school-list

Splawn, M. (2022, December 27). *10 Essential cooking skills that every cook should know.* The Spruce Eats. https://www.thespruceeats.com/essential-cooking-skills-to-know-6743595

Stanford, C. (2014, July 5). *Adapting communication styles to different audiences.* Fleximize. https://fleximize.com/articles/000592/communication-styles

Steves, R. (n.d.). *Do I need travel insurance?* Rick Steves Europe. https://www.rick steves.com/travel-tips/trip-planning/travel-insurance

Taking charge of your medical care (for teens). (n.d.). KidsHealth. https://kidshealth. org/en/teens/medical-care.html

10 Driving tips for new drivers. (2021, April 1). Bridgestone. https://www.bridge stonetire.ca/learn/maintenance/10-driving-tips-for-new-drivers/

10 Tips to help your adolescent find balance in the digital age. (n.d.). Silicon Valley International School. https://blog.siliconvalleyinternational.org/10-tips-to-help-your-adolescent-find-balance-in-the-digital-age

10 Tips to improve your mental health. (n.d.). Elumind Centres. https://elumind.com/10-tips-to-improve-your-mental-health/?gclid

10 Ways you can help fight the climate crisis. (2022, May 4). UN Environment

Programme; UNEP. https://www.unep.org/news-and-stories/story/10-ways-you-can-help-fight-climate-crisis

The difference between a lease and a rental agreement. (2019, January 23). TransUnion SmartMove. https://www.mysmartmove.com/blog/difference-between-lease-and-rental-agreement

The most important travel documents for your trip. (2022, September 26). Iata. https://www.iata.org/en/publications/newsletters/iata-knowledge-hub/the-most-important-travel-documents-for-your-trip/

Thompson, D. (2019, July 22). *Few teens are prepared to handle adult life skills, poll finds.* UPI. https://www.upi.com/Health_News/2019/07/22/Few-teens-are-prepared-to-handle-adult-life-skills-poll-finds/2191563818390/

Travel insurance and safety for travelers. (n.d.). Arrive Alive. https://www.arrivealive.mobi/travel-insurance-and-safety-for-travellers

TurboTax. (2023, November 28). *A guide to commonly-used IRS tax forms.* Intuit Turbotax. https://turbotax.intuit.com/tax-tips/irs-tax-forms/a-guide-to-commonly-used-irs-tax-forms/L7YJv3Sbh

Twelve tips to reduce, reuse & recycle. (n.d.). City of Whitewater. https://www.whitewater-wi.gov/241/Twelve-Tips-to-Reduce-Reuse-Recycle

Twenge, J. M. (2017, September). *Have smartphones destroyed a generation?* The Atlantic. https://www.theatlantic.com/magazine/archive/2017/09/has-the-smartphone-destroyed-a-generation/534198/

20 Ways to showcase your experience on your resume. (n.d.). Augustana University. https://www.augie.edu/academics/student-success-center/services-students/resources-finding-job-or-internship/20-ways

Ultimate guide: Copper's guide to budgeting (for teens). (n.d.). Copper. https://www.getcopper.com/guide/budgeting

University of Waterloo. (n.d.). *Effective communication: Barriers and strategies.* University of Waterloo. https://uwaterloo.ca/centre-for-teaching-excellence/catalogs/tip-sheets/effective-communication-barriers-and-strategies

What is a FICO Score and why is it important? (n.d.). MyFICO. https://www.myfico.com/credit-education/what-is-a-fico-score

What is a lease? (2022, April 28). Settlement.org. https://settlement.org/ontario/housing/rent-a-home/apply-for-rental-housing/what-is-a-lease/#:

What is renters insurance? (n.d.). Nationwide. https://www.nationwide.com/lc/resources/home/articles/what-is-renters-insurance#:

What should I keep in my first aid kit? (2021, April 7). NHS. https://www.nhs.uk/common-health-questions/accidents-first-aid-and-treatments/what-should-i-keep-in-my-first-aid-kit/

What to have in your car emergency kit. (n.d.). Aaa. https://www.aaa.com/autorepair/articles/what-to-have-in-your-car-emergency-kit

White, J. (2022, May 14). *Why is it important to establish credit when young?* Experian. https://www.experian.com/blogs/ask-experian/why-it-is-important-to-estab lish-credit-when-you-are-young/#:

Whiteside, E. (2023, October 10). *What is the 50/20/30 budget rule?* Investopedia. https://www.investopedia.com/ask/answers/022916/what-502030-budget-rule.asp

Why student internships are important for career development. (2023, May 15). 1Mentor. https://www.1mentor.io/blog-posts-1mentor/why-student-internships-important-career-development

Wilson, B. (2023, July 15). *Discomfort: A pathway to growth.* Psychology Today. https://www.psychologytoday.com/ca/blog/explorations-in-positive-psychol ogy/202307/discomfort-a-pathway-to-growth

Wilson, C. (2021, October 29). *How to improve your empathic listening skills: 7 Techniques.* Positive Psychology. https://positivepsychology.com/empathic-listening/

Zaremba, J. (2022, January 7). *Why get a passport? 10 great reasons.* GoAbroad. https://www.goabroad.com/articles/benefits-of-a-passport

www.ingramcontent.com/pod-product-compliance
Lightning Source LLC
Chambersburg PA
CBHW060547160726
47991CB00001B/464